BAKING COOKBOOK FOR TEENAGERS

Cook Baker

TABLE OF CONTENTS

RAINBOW PIZZAS 67

PIZZA ROLLS 68

PIZZA WITH HOMEMADE SAUCE 69

TUNA, OLIVE & ROCKET PIZZAS 70

MOZZARELLA, HAM & PESTO PIZZAS 71

CHEESE & BACON SCONE PIZZA 72

TUNA MELT PIZZA BAGUETTES 73

CHORIZO AND SPANISH BLACK OLIVE PIZZA 74

SMOKED AUBERGINE AND BURRATA PIZZA 75

HOMEMADE PEPPERONI PIZZA 76

ONION AND RED PEPPER PIZZA 77

BACON, ASPARAGUS AND GOAT CHEESE PIZZA 78

PIZZA ALLA NAPOLETANA 79

PORCINI PIZZA 80

HEDGEHOG ROLLS 81

EASY BREAD 82

FLOWERPOT BREAD 83

CHEESY GARLIC BAGUETTE 84

CHEESE & PESTO WHIRLS 85

CHEESE ROLL-UPS 86

TIGER BREAD 87

TRIANGULAR BREAD THINS 88

CHEESY BONFIRE BREAD 89

EASY BREAD ROLLS 90

MEATBALL & GARLIC BREAD TRAYBAKE 91

NAAN BREAD 92

VEGAN BANANA BREAD 93

PEACH BREAD 94

PUMPKIN BREAD 95

ZUCCHINI BREAD 96

PAN DE MUERTOS 97

BUTTERMILK BREAD RECIPE WITH HONEY 98

EASY SODA BREAD 99

FOCACCIA 100

POTATO & TURMERIC FOCACCIA 101

FOCACCIA WITH PESTO & MOZZARELLA 102

ARTICHOKE FOCACCIA 103

PESTO FOCACCIA SANDWICH 104

PITTA BREAD 105

CARAMELISED ONION FOCACCIA 106

RED ONION & ROSEMARY FOCACCIA 107

INTRODUCTION TO BAKING COOKBOOK FOR TEENAGERS

Pastries are some of the most consumed snacks or desserts that people have all around the world. You might have contributed to the number of people who make up this statistic. Apparently, for every time you had a pastry, you must have wondered how someone could have mixed different ingredients into a box of yummy, delicious, mouthwatering pastry that leaves your taste bud asking for more. For you to be reading this book, you probably need answers; indeed, this book contains all the answers that you possibly need.In this chapter, we will take you through the basics of baking, the equipment you need, and the basic rules that you should follow. Let's get started!

WHY BAKING?

Baking is a cooking method that requires the use of dry heat from the oven or any other improvised method that provides such dry heat. Other cooking methods include frying, baking, steaming, stewing, smoking, grilling, roasting, among others. When it comes to pastries, baking seems to be the best cooking method that delivers the best result.

You might think that all baking has to offer is a ready-made pastry, but it has a lot more to offer. As teenagers, you are probably becoming more conscious of what you eat, your body shape, and the extent of calories that you consume. Learning to bake yourself affords you the opportunity to not only get to make your pastry yourself, but you also get to make it to suit your taste and your health needs. Baking also allows you to bond with your friends and create memories with them.

When you want to bake, you can easily have your friend over to join you in the process. This means more time to be productive as friends, and more time to stay together, catching on the entire gist you have long desired to share with them. Moreover, baking reaches out to the depth of creativity in you. You can bake your pastry into any shape, size, or model it after any character or object that you love the most. Likewise, pastries are one of the consumables that are in high demand, and people are willing to pay others to make it for them. This could mean extra cash for you if you can bake for other people.

Sometimes you are confused about what to gift your friend on their birthdays. You could make them an incredibly beautiful cake that would make their day. No one says "No" to a nicely backed and well-designed cake. Moreover, when you are out on a picnic or hangout with your friends, you could make all the pastries, saving you the cost that would have gone into buying such pastries from a store. The beauty in this is that while having time out as friends, there are fresh pastries to keep the fun going.

With baking, you could become a celebrity! At one time or the other, you must have seen other people post the things they do on Instagram, Facebook and Youtube. With their posts, they gain extremely high followers. You too can post the videos of your baking escapades on the social media and earn a good number of followers. You really might not have to be worried about the content of your next video. All you need to do is to try baking something nice and getting others to see. Consistently doing this earns you the celebrity status on a platter of gold.

Besides other things that baking can afford you when you gain mastery in baking (as you consistently bake and get really good at it), you stand a chance to become a pastry chef. It does not matter that you are young, what matters is that you wield a good knowledge in the art of baking and you can put it to use to get amazing world-class results all the time. The idea of a teenage pastry chef is one that is worthy of aspiring to, and you should aspire to it.

WHY A BAKING COOKBOOK

Every time you craved your favorite pastry, you probably had to make an order online and wait for some time for it to be delivered. At other times, it might have happened that you suddenly started craving a pastry at night when the stores have closed, and you could not make your order; so, you had to wait till the next day before you could satisfy your craving.

These andmany more are the likely situations that may occur when you love pastries but do not know how to make them. This explains why you need a baking cookbook, and if you are reading this, you have one already.With a baking cookbook, you have a "do it yourself" knowledge that can take you through a baking process successfully. The feeling is not different from having your tutor by your side to help you understand and solve your mathematical problems. A baking cookbook is your tutor and a chef standing by you, helping you every step of the way.

Usually, cookbooks provide you with a list of ingredients required for any form of baking you want to do. This does not exclude the minute detail about the heat required and the quantity of the ingredients that you need.

When it comes to baking, there are no limits; you can come up with new recipes and try out on improving the ones you already know. A cookbook can also take you through this process. You can become a master at cooking to the point that you can effortlessly try out new recipes and still get really amazing results

EQUIPMENTS NECESSARY FOR BAKING

Just as it applies in every fteld of life, there are equipment and tools that are required for baking. Here is a list of all that you would need as regards baking:

• THE OVEN: An oven is to a baker what a stethoscope is to a doctor. It's about the most important equipment in baking. After making your dough or barter, you need an equipment to heat it up and make it into the ready-to-consume pastry;

the oven is that equipment that does that job. It is very possible that you don't own an electric oven, yet you want to bake. In this instance, you might find other alternatives such as preheating a pot or using the manual oven attached to your gas cooker to serve this purpose. However, it is advisable to get an electric oven that has a thermometer because it controls the heat better than the manual oven. Too much heat can make your pastry too hard. This is why heat control must come with a level of precision, and an oven provides you with that.

- **MEASURING CUPS AND SPOONS:** Measurement is everything in baking. There is hardly any ingredient in baking that does not require measurement, whether wet or dry. Yet, accuracy in measurement could make all the difference in baking a pastry. Too much of anything can ruin the entire outcome; too much flour can make your pasty too dry and not fluffy, too much sugar or salt can ruin the taste too. That's where measuring cups and spoons come in handy. Measuring cups come in different sizes ranging from ¼ to 1 with and about 4 to 6 cups making up a set. Measuring spoons on the other hand range from ¼ teaspoon to 1 tablespoon.

MIXER: Mixing your ingredients is a core in baking; not just mixing but mixing to the right texture. A mixer helps you get by the initial and even the entire process of making your dough or barter. For beginners, a hand mixer is a good option because you are just getting started and you probably don't have so much to bake at a time. However, as you master the art and when you have more to do; a standing mixer or an electric mixer is a better option. It saves you the stress of having to make your barter in bits and can beat it to the right texture that you desire. Among other things, a mixer will help you beat your butter till it becomes creamy, knead your dough, whip your eggs, and of course make your barter in no time.

- FOOD SCALE: One disaster you should be itching to prevent at all cost is having too much of any ingredient in your barter or dough. It can mess up the entire process for you. A food scale helps you to keep that in check. The difference between a food scale and measuring cups and spoons is that a food scale measures in grams, which is more accurate. Also, a food scale is perfect for measuring dry ingredients. Baking is a game of precision, and a food scale checks that box.

MIXING BOWLS: It is extremely easy for you to ignore getting a set of mixing bowls, but you really should not. There are other bowls you already have that could serve this purpose, but you might still need mixing bowls. Mixing bowls help you have a smooth process when it comes to mixing your barter or dough. It is easier to clean up your mixing bowls after use because they are made from stainless steel. In choosing your mixing bowls, stay away from aluminum products because acidic ingredient (like vinegar, depending on the type you are using) might react with the metal and can change the flavor of your pastry.

BAKING PANS: Baking can be as creative as you want it to be. You can have your pastry in whatever shape you desire; heart shape, square, triangle or have it in a number based on your preference. You have probably seen multilayered cakes too. Baking pan gives a variety of shapes that make them up. Baking pans are the tools you need to do all the shape magic you want. Besides making your pastry take shape, the barter or dough are usually put in a baking pan when it is time to bake. Baking pans come in different sizes, ranging from size six to size twelve.

SPATULA: A spatula comes in handy when you need to scoop your barter into the baking pan and can also be used when frosting. Also, when you need to make really smooth edges while designing your cake or any other pastry you have made, a spatula is the tool required. A spatula can be an offset spatula or a silicone spatula. An offset spatula can be used for decorating your cakes and can also be used to remove the ready-made pastry from the pan. A silicone spatula, on the other hand, can be used to scoop the barter into the pan completely and neatly. Rather than mess up your hand while decorating, scooping, or frosting, a spatula is a choice you should make.

- **ROLLING PIN:** Rolling pins are a must-have when you are making a dough. Rolling pins are primarily used for rolling out dough and flattening them out.

- They are useful when you need to make your pies, pizza dough and even cookies. Rolling pins are generally about 25cm to 40 cm long and 5-71/2 cm in diameter. Hardwood rolling pins are the most common types of rolling pins. On the occasion where you don't own one, you could improvise using old bottles that are round in shape to serve the same purpose.

- **PASTRY AND COOKIE CUTTERS:** Baking can be as much fun as you
want it to be. At different times, you might want to try out your creativity while baking a pastry; a pastry cutter helps you do that. A pastry cutter helps you shape your dough into desired shapes, and it does it perfectly leaving no rough edges on the dough. At other, it gives really fine and perfect shape and size you want to make your dough into. You probably have seen your pizza in that rectangular shape many times; a pastry cutter did that.

- **PASTRY BRUSH:** There are seemingly easy tasks in baking that require you to oil your hands and also requires your hand to be really neat (glazing your dough and oiling your pans are good examples). A pastry brush comes in handy in doing these tasks. With a baking brush, you can oil your baking pan effectively and even reach the edges your fingers can't get to. When glazing your dough with an egg mixture or milk, a pastry brush does it better because it gives the thin layer of glaze that is required without dipping the dough into the glazing agent.

MIX: A Mix is used to beat some wet ingredients. For instance, if you need to beat three eggs, you might use your fork, but when you need to beat about six eggs and more, you will need a Mix to do it better than a fork would. A Mix could be used to whip air into wet ingredients that you need in baking so that they can get fluffy, frosty, or beat them into the texture that is perfect for the purpose you need them for.

- **COOLING RACK:** The cooling process of your pastry is as important as the whole process. Any extra heat after removing your pastry from the oven can mess up the ready-made pastry. It can also alter the texture of your pastry, making it hard rather than fluffy. That is why you need a cooling rack. A cooling rack helps your pastry cool evenly without making any alteration to it. It exposes it to enough air evenly and makes it ready to serve in no time.

- **SIFTER:** A sifter is mainly used for dry ingredients like flour, sugar, baking powder, cocoa powder etc. The sifter helps rid these ingredients of possible lumps they might contain. In other instances, it is possible you want to use the leftovers of those ingredients. A sifter helps separate insects or any other dirt that might have gone into them. You can easily get a powdered ingredient that your baking requires after running it through the sifter.

SIMPLE BAKING RULES

Baking is a world on its own and has a lot to offer when it comes to exploring new creative and innovative ideas. However, baking has some rules that should be obeyed and lines that should not be crossed. Flouting kitchen rules could yield really fatal results; your pastry could turn out bad, an accident may occur, and you might even get yourself injured. Hence, you must abide by the rules, not only for what you are baking but also for yourself.

1) The ftrst thing to do when you want to bake is to clear the kitchen and make it ready for baking. You should clean the tabletop and sweep the floor just to ensure that the kitchen is as clean as it can possibly be.

2) Prepare all Appliances: Before you begin to bake, you should take out all the appliances that you would need to use. You should ensure you check all the wires and the plugs to ensure they are in good condition. After checking, you should clean all the appliances and prepare them for use. Some of the appliances may require you to wash them, e.g. the mixing bowl, spatulas etc.

3) The ftrst thing to do when you want to bake is to clear the kitchen and make it ready for baking. You should clean the tabletop and sweep the floor just to ensure that the kitchen is as clean as it can possibly be.

4) Prepare all Appliances: Before you begin to bake, you should take out all the appliances that you would need to use. You should ensure you check all the wires and the plugs to ensure they are in good condition. After checking, you should clean all the appliances and prepare them for use. Some of the appliances may require you to wash them, e.g. the mixing bowl, spatulas etc.

5) Before you begin baking, ensure you wear an apron to keep yourself clean. You don't want to get yourself stained with every ingredient you used while baking. You should also wear a cap that would cover all of your hair to avoid your hair from getting into what you are baking.

6) Clear the tools and equipment as you use them: You might need to use sharp objects like knives, beaters forks, among other things. This equipment has a tendency to get you injured. So, when you are done with those objects, take them off the tabletop. Likewise, as you progress in your baking, clean up! Clean all spills on the floor to avoid falling or any bodily injury.

7) Be mindful of the equipment: Baking equipment requires that you constantly check them as you make use of them. However, while trying to check them, avoid using your bare hand.

8) Ensure you keep a ftre extinguisher in the kitchen close. Fire accident can occur while you are baking. A ftre extinguisher helps you put out the ftre in no time before it gets out of hand.

9) Ensure you put off all electrical appliances when you are done using them.

10) Once you are done with baking, wash all appliances that you used, disconnect all electrical appliances, and place them back safely in their packs. Do well to switch off all sockets too. Besides kitchen rules that you need to obey, there are baking rules that you should not ignore too. Some of these baking rules are:

- BE MINDFUL OF MEASUREMENT: Measurement in baking is everything. A lot could go wrong if the rule of measurement is not obeyed, and that is why you need to be accurate with measurement. Hence, while measuring your ingredients, ensure you have the exact quantity of what you need. If you are not sure or you think you have made a mistake, start the measuring process all over again. It is better to err on the path of caution.

- While using any electronic equipment, don't stick your hand into them while they are in use. Do not put your hand into the mixer while mixing; do not put your bare hand in the oven while it is hot. Doing that could get you injured

- Wash your hands regularly while baking. You might have to touch dirty surfaces while baking yet you need to flatten out your dough. A dirty hand could contaminate the dough.

- Ensure you use the correct oven temperature while baking. Too much heat could ruin the entire process. This might mean that you need to monitor the heat at intervals.

- Ensure you clean up the equipment you used when you are done baking.

Chocolate Chip Cup Mug

TIME TO PREPARE
5 minutes

COOK TIME
4 minutes

SERVING
1 People

PREPARED BY
Cook Baker

Ingredients

- ✓ 4 tbsp all purpose flour
- ✓ 2 tbsp brown sugar
- ✓ 1/4 tsp baking powder
- ✓ 3 tbsp low fat milk
- ✓ 1/8 tsp vanilla
- ✓ 1/2 tbsp vegetable oil
- ✓ 2 tbsp semisweet chocolate chips

Steps to Cook

1. Merge all ingredients except chocolate chips into a microwave safe mug. This is a small cake so you can use an 8 oz mug and it should just reach the top when finished cooking. You can also use
an oversized mug, but the cake will be lower in the mug. Mix with
a small, sturdy Mix until a smooth batter forms and no lumps remain.

2. Stir in half of the chocolate chips. Sprinkle remaining half over surface. Cook in microwave for about 1 minute. Let cool a few minutes before eating.

Flourless Peanut Butter Mug Cake

TIME TO PREPARE

5 minutes

COOK TIME

4 minutes

SERVING

1 People

PREPARED BY

Cook Baker

Ingredients

- ✓ 2 tbsp peanut butter *creamy*
- ✓ 1/8 tsp baking powder
- ✓ 1 tbsp white granulated sugar
- ✓ 1 large egg

Steps to Cook

1   Mix all ingredients into an oversized, microwave-safe mug until batter is smooth. Microwave for about 1 minute. Let cake cool a few minutes before eating.

Cinnamon Roll Mug

TIME TO PREPARE
5 minutes

COOK TIME
4 minutes

SERVING
1 People

PREPARED BY
Cook Baker

Ingredients

- ✓ 4 tbsp all purpose flour
- ✓ 2 tbsp brown sugar
- ✓ 1/4 tsp baking powder
- ✓ 3 tbsp low fat milk
- ✓ 1/8 tsp vanilla
- ✓ 1/2 tbsp vegetable oil
- ✓ 2 tbsp semisweet chocolate chips

Steps to Cook

1. Merge all ingredients except chocolate chips into a microwave safe mug. This is a small cake so you can use an 8 oz mug and it should just reach the top when finished cooking. You can also use an oversized mug, but the cake will be lower in the mug. Mix with a small, sturdy Mix until a smooth batter forms and no lumps remain.

2. Stir in half of the chocolate chips. Sprinkle remaining half over surface. Cook in microwave for about 1 minute. Let cool a few minutes before eating.

Dark Chocolate Chip Cookies

TIME TO PREPARE

5 minutes

COOK TIME

4 minutes

SERVING

1 People

PREPARED BY

Cook Baker

Ingredients

- 1 cup unsalted cold butter *cut into small cubes*
- 1 cup packed light brown sugar
- ½ cup granulated white sugar
- large eggs
- ½ cup dark unsweetened cocoa powder *try to use a premium brand for richer flavor*
- 1 cup cake flour
- 1½ cup all-purpose flour
- 1 tsp cornstarch
- ¾ tsp baking soda
- ½ tsp salt
- cup semisweet chocolate chunks or roughly chopped chocolate
- 1/2 cup semisweet chocolate chips

Steps to Cook

1. Preheat oven to 410°F.

2. In a mixing bowl of a stand mixer, cream together butter and sugars on high speed until light and fluffy (about 3-4 minutes). Add eggs one at a time, mixing well after each addition.

3. Add in cocoa, cake flour, all-purpose flour, cornstarch, baking soda, and salt and set mixer on lowest speed setting to stir until dough is just Merged (please note in the video the mixing is sped up to keep the video short). You want the dough to be smooth and uniform in color, but you don't want to overmix it. Stir in chocolate chunks.

4. Place the dough in the fridge for 15 minutes to chill.

5. Line two baking sheets with silicone baking mats. Measure out about 4.3 oz of dough and roll into a ball. Place several chocolate chips on top and adjust chips until the dough weighs 4.5 oz. Place dough ball onto baking sheet. You will place four on each baking sheet, spaced about 2 inches apart.

6. You should have enough dough to make 8 cookies, but it is best to weigh the balls so that they are all the same size and will cook evenly.

7. Bake the cookies for about 10-11 minutes, or until the surface is dry and cookies look almost set. Remove and let cookies cool on the baking sheets (if you try to remove them they will likely break apart). Allow cookies to cool about 15-20 minutes so that they can set. Then remove and enjoy.

Nutella Brownies

TIME TO PREPARE

5 minutes

COOK TIME

15 minutes

SERVING

1 People

PREPARED BY

Cook Baker

Ingredients

- ✓ 1/4 cup Nutella
- ✓ large eggs
- ✓ 1/2 cup all purpose flour

Steps to Cook

1. Preheat oven to 350°F. Grease a 9 inch x 9 inch metal baking pan. Add all ingredients into a large bowl and mix until batter is smooth. Pour into baking pan and smooth top with spatula.

2. Bake for about 15 minutes until toothpick inserted comes out clean. Be careful not to bake too long otherwise brownies will dry out. Let brownies cool and set before cutting and serving.

Blueberry Scones

TIME TO PREPARE
5 minutes

COOK TIME
15 minutes

SERVING
1 People

PREPARED BY
Cook Baker

Ingredients

✓ cups (250g) all-purpose flour (spoon & leveled), plus more for hands and work surface

✓ 1/2 cup (100g) granulated sugar

✓ and 1/2 teaspoons baking powder

✓ 1 teaspoon ground cinnamon

✓ 1/2 teaspoon salt

✓ 1/2 cup (1 stick; 115g) unsalted butter, frozen

✓ 1/2 cup (120ml) heavy cream (plus 2 Tbsp for brushing)

✓ 1 large egg

✓ 1 and 1/2 teaspoons pure vanilla extract

✓ 1 heaping cup (180g) fresh or frozen blueberries (do not thaw)

✓ for topping: coarse sugar and vanilla icing

Steps to Cook

1. Mix flour, sugar, baking powder, cinnamon, and salt together in a large bowl. Grate the frozen butter using a box grater. Add it to the flour mixture and Merge with a pastry cutter, two forks, or your fingers until the mixture comes together in pea-sized crumbs. See video above for a closer look at the texture. Place in the refrigerator or freezer as you mix the wet ingredients together.

2. Mix 1/2 cup heavy cream, the egg, and vanilla extract together in a small bowl. Drizzle over the flour mixture, add the blueberries, then mix together until everything appears moistened.

3. Pour onto the counter and, with floured hands, work dough into a ball as best you can. Dough will be sticky. If it's too sticky, add a little more flour. If it seems too dry, add 1-2 more Tablespoons heavy cream. Press into an 8-inch disc and, with a sharp knife or bench scraper, cut into 8 wedges.

4. Brush scones with remaining heavy cream and for extra crunch, sprinkle with coarse sugar. (You can do this before or after refrigerating in the next step.)

5. Place scones on a plate or lined baking sheet (if your fridge has space!) and refrigerate for at least 15 minutes.

6. Meanwhile, preheat oven to 400°F (204°C).

7. Line a large baking sheet with parchment paper or silicone baking mat. After refrigerating, arrange scones 2-3 inches apart on the prepared baking sheet(s).

8. Bake for 22-25 minutes or until golden brown around the edges and lightly browned on top. Remove from the oven and cool for a few minutes before topping with vanilla icing.

9. Leftover iced or un-iced scones keep well at room temperature for 2 days or in the refrigerator for 5 days.

Peanut Butter Pie

TIME TO PREPARE
20 minutes

COOK TIME
20 minutes

SERVING
2 People

PREPARED BY
Marie Austin

Ingredients

- **Oreo Crust**
- ✓ 24 **peanut butter Oreos** (or regular, Double Stuf is ok!)
- ✓ 5 Tablespoons (75g) **unsalted butter**, melted
- **Ganache**
- ✓ 3/4 cup (180g) **heavy cream**
- ✓ 6 ounces (170g) **semi-sweet chocolate**, coarsely chopped
- **Peanut Butter Filling**
- ✓ 3/4 cup (180ml) **heavy cream**
- ✓ 8 ounce (224g) block **cream cheese**, softened to room temperature
- ✓ 1 and 1/2 cups (310g) creamy **peanut butter**
- ✓ 3/4 cup (90g) **confectioners' sugar**
- ✓ 1 teaspoon **pure vanilla extract**
- ✓ 1 cup (200g) **Reese's Pieces**, crushed

Steps to Cook

1. Preheat the oven to 350°F (177°C). Spray a 9-inch pie dish with nonstick spray or grease lightly with butter.

2. **Make the crust:** In a food processor or blender, pulse the whole Oreos into a fine crumb. Stir the cookie crumbs and melted butter together, then press into the pie dish. Bake for 9-10 minutes. Allow to cool as you prepare the rest.

3. **Make the ganache:** Place chopped chocolate in a medium bowl. Heat the cream in a small saucepan over medium heat, stirring occasionally. Once it begins to boil, immediately remove from heat then pour over the chocolate. Stir gently until the ganache is smooth. Set aside and allow to cool to room temperature. During this time, it will slowly thicken as well.

4. **Make the filling:** Using a hand mixer or a stand mixer fitted with a Mix attachment, beat the heavy cream on medium-high speed until stiff peaks form, about 5 minutes. Spoon the whipped cream into a bowl and set aside. Using the same mixing bowl (no need to rinse clean!), beat the cream cheese, peanut butter, confectioners' sugar, and vanilla extract together on medium-high speed until Merged. Mixture will be thick. Fold in the whipped cream until smooth. be gentle, you don't want to deflate that cream.

5. Sprinkle half of the Reese's Pieces on top of the cooled crust. Spread peanut butter filling evenly on top, then spread ganache on top of filling. Sprinkle the rest of the Reese's Pieces on top.

6. Chill the pie in the refrigerator for 5-6 hours or even overnight. Slice and serve cold.

Colored Leaf Cookies

TIME TO PREPARE
30 minutes

COOK TIME
15 minutes

SERVING
1 People

PREPARED BY
Cook Baker

Ingredients

- ✓ tubes sugar cookie dough
- ✓ 1/4 c. flour
- ✓ Red, yellow, orange, and green food coloring

Steps to Cook

1. Preheat oven to 350.
2. Place the cookie dough into a large bowl and mix together with the flour.
3. Divide the dough into four separate bowls. Dye each piece of dough a different color with the food dye, until you are satisfied with the colors.
4. In a large bowl Merge all doughs. Onto a lightly floured surface using a rolling pin, roll out dough to about 1/2" thick and cut leaves out with cookie cutters. Place on parchment lined baking sheets about an inch apart and bake for 8-10 minutes, or until slightly golden on the edges. Let cool and serve.

Owl Cupcakes

TIME TO PREPARE

20 minutes

COOK TIME

70 minutes

SERVING

24 Cupcake

PREPARED BY

Marie Austin

Ingredients

- ✓ 1 box chocolate cake batter, plus ingredients called for on box
- ✓ 1 (16-oz.) tub chocolate frosting
- ✓ 24 Oreos, halved
- ✓ 48 chocolate mini M&Ms
- ✓ 24 orange mini M&Ms

Steps to Cook

1. Preheat oven to 350º and line 2 12-cup muffin tins with black cupcake liners. Prepare cupcake batter according to package directions.

2. Scoop cupcake batter into liners and bake until a toothpick inserted in the center comes out clean, 22 to 25 minutes. Let cool.

3. Frost cupcakes with chocolate frosting, making two swooshes on top for ears!

4. Top with Oreo halves, icing side up for eyes. Dot the bottom of chocolate mini M&Ms with frosting and place on top of Oreo halves for eyeballs.

5. Place an orange mini M&M for the nose.

Pencil Sugar Cookies

TIME TO PREPARE	**SERVING**
20 minutes	24 Pencils
COOK TIME	**PREPARED BY**
20 minutes	Cook Baker

Ingredients

- ✓ 24 sugar wafer cookies
- ✓ 1 1/2 c. white chocolate chips
- ✓ 1 tbsp. coconut oil
- ✓ pink food coloring
- ✓ mini chocolate chips

Steps to Cook

1. Line a large baking sheet with parchment paper. Using a small serrated knife, make two diagonal cuts into one end of each wafer cookie to create a point.

2. In a microwave safe bowl, microwave white chocolate chips at 50% power in 30 second intervals until melted. Mix in coconut oil then separate into two bowls.

3. To one bowl of melted white chocolate, Mix in a couple drops of pink food coloring.

4. Dip the flat end of each cookie into the pink chocolate to create the eraser, then dip the pointed end of each cookie into the white chocolate to make the tip. Place a mini chocolate chip at the point of each pencil.

5. Let sit for 15 minutes, or until set.

Homemade Pancakes

TIME TO PREPARE
10 minutes

COOK TIME
12 minutes

SERVING
3 People

PREPARED BY
Cook Baker

Ingredients

- ✓ 1 cup all-purpose flour
- ✓ 2 tablespoons sugar
- ✓ 2 teaspoons baking powder
- ✓ 1/2 teaspoon salt
- ✓ 1 large egg (slightly beaten)
- ✓ 2 tablespoons vegetable oil
- ✓ 3/4 cup milk

Steps to Cook

1. Gather the ingredients.
2. Merge the flour, sugar, baking powder, and salt. Mix or stir to blend thoroughly.
3. Stir in egg, oil, and the milk. Mix lightly, just enough to blend.
4. When ready to cook, grease a griddle with butter.
5. Using a 1/4 cup measuring scoop, measure out pancakes onto the griddle to cook.
6. Cook the pancakes, flipping them when you see bubbles breaking all over the tops.
7. Continue cooking until the underside is browned.
8. Serve and enjoy.

Apple Dump Cake

TIME TO PREPARE
15 minutes

COOK TIME
45 minutes

SERVING
16 People

PREPARED BY
Marie Austin

Ingredients

- ✓ 5 medium apples (peeled, cored and sliced)
- ✓ 1 cup chopped nuts of your choice (lightly toasted)
- ✓ 4 teaspoons cinnamon (divided)
- ✓ 1 teaspoon freshly ground nutmeg
- ✓ 1/2 cup sugar
- ✓ 1 1/4 cup apple cider (or apple juice)
- ✓ 1 (18-ounce) box yellow cake mix
- ✓ 3/4 cup butter (melted)

Steps to Cook

1. Preheat oven to 375 F. Lightly grease a 9 x 13-inch pan.

2. In the pan, mix apples and nuts with 2 teaspoons cinnamon, nutmeg, and sugar.

3. Spread evenly in the pan and cover with apple cider.

4. Sprinkle dry cake mix over apple mixture. Sprinkle with remaining cinnamon.

5. Pour melted butter over top.

6. Bake for 45 minutes or until golden brown and bubbly.

7. Serve and enjoy!

Rice Crispy Treats

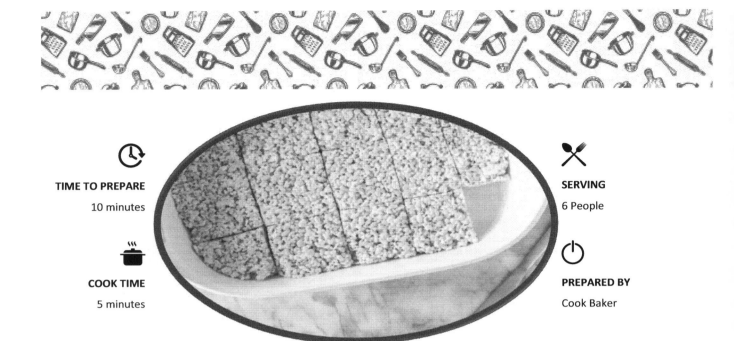

TIME TO PREPARE
10 minutes

COOK TIME
5 minutes

SERVING
6 People

PREPARED BY
Cook Baker

Ingredients

- ✓ 6 cups crispy rice cereal
- ✓ 3 tablespoons butter
- ✓ 4 cups mini marshmallows (or 10 ounces regular marshmallows)

Steps to Cook

1. Spray a heat-proof spatula and a 9 x 13 pan or jellyroll pan with cooking spray.
2. In a small saucepan, melt the butter and marshmallows over low heat, stirring frequently until the marshmallows are completely melted.
3. Pour over the crispy rice cereal.
4. Toss with the spatula to coat the cereal well.
5. Immediately transfer the rice crispy treats mixture to the prepared pan, and spread into an even layer with the spatula.
6. Let rice crispy treats cool completely before cutting into squares.
7. Serve and enjoy!

Blueberry Muffins

TIME TO PREPARE

12 minutes

COOK TIME

20 minutes

SERVING

12 People

PREPARED BY

Cook Baker

Ingredients

- ✓ 7 tablespoons unsalted butter (melted and cooled)
- ✓ 2/3 cup sugar
- ✓ large eggs
- ✓ 2/3 cup milk
- ✓ 1 1/2 teaspoons vanilla extract
- ✓ 1/4 teaspoon almond extract
- ✓ cups (9 ounces) all-purpose flour
- ✓ teaspoons baking powder
- ✓ 1/4 teaspoon baking soda
- ✓ 1/2 teaspoon salt
- ✓ 1 1/2 cups blueberries (fresh or frozen)
- ✓ 1 tablespoon sugar (mixed with 1/2 teaspoon cinnamon or 1/4 teaspoon vanilla extract)

Steps to Cook

2. Generously grease 12 muffin cups or spray with nonstick cooking spray or baking spray.
3. Heat the oven to 375 F.
4. In the bowl of an electric mixer, Merge the melted butter and sugar. Beat until smooth and well blended. Beat in the eggs, then slowly beat in the milk and vanilla and almond extracts.
5. In another bowl, Merge the flour with the baking powder, soda, and salt. Slowly beat into the first mixture until well blended.
6. With a spoon or rubber spatula, gently fold in the blueberries.
7. Fill the prepared muffin cups about 2/3 full. For uniform muffins, use a 1/4-cup scoop or measuring cup to measure the batter.
8. If desired, sprinkle with a mixture of 1 tablespoon of sugar and about 1/2 teaspoon of cinnamon. Or sprinkle a little vanilla sugar over the muffins.
9. Bake for 18 to 21 minutes, or until the muffins are lightly browned and a toothpick comes out clean when inserted into the center of a muffin.
10. Let cool in the pan on a rack for 10 minutes. Using a butter knife, carefully loosen the muffins from the muffin cups and remove to a rack to cool completely. Serve right away or freeze the cooled muffins on a rack or sheet pan then transfer to freezer bags and label. Thaw at room temperature or heat in the microwave or oven.
11. To reheat the frozen muffins, place an unwrapped muffin on a paper towel or paper plate and microwave on full power for about 25 to 30 seconds.
12. To reheat frozen muffins in the oven, wrap in foil and heat at 350 F for about 10 to 15 minutes.

Easy Thumbprint Cookies

TIME TO PREPARE

30 minutes

COOK TIME

10 minutes

SERVING

6 People

PREPARED BY

Cook Baker

Ingredients

- ✓ 1/2 cup unsalted butter (softened)
- ✓ 3/4 cup sugar
- ✓ 1 egg (lightly beaten)
- ✓ 1 1/2 cups all-purpose flour
- ✓ 1/2 teaspoon baking powder
- ✓ 1/2 teaspoon salt
- ✓ 1 cup almonds (ground)
- ✓ 1/2 teaspoon vanilla extract
- ✓ 1/2 cup of strawberry jam

Steps to Cook

1. Preheat the oven to 350 F.
2. Lightly grease a baking sheet and set aside.
3. Using an electric mixer, cream together the butter and sugar until pale and fluffy—for about 2 minutes. Add the egg and continue to mix until Merged and smooth.
4. In a large bowl, sift together the flour, baking powder, and salt. Add about 1/2 cup of flour mixture to the butter mixture, stirring continuously with a wooden spoon until smooth. Add the remaining flour mixture and stir until smooth.
5. Add the ground almonds and vanilla essence and stir until Merged.
6. Roll small balls of dough and place them on the baking sheet about 1 inch (2.5cm) apart. Dip your thumb in some flour and then gently press down on the dough to make well in the middle of each cookie. Spoon a small amount of jam into each well. Bake the cookies for 10 minutes or until they are a light golden color. Remove from oven and cool on a wire rack. Serve.
7. Store cookies in an airtight container for up to 2 weeks.

Marshmallow Flower Cookies

TIME TO PREPARE
15 minutes

COOK TIME
30 minutes

SERVING
10 People

PREPARED BY
Cook Baker

Ingredients

- ✓ (16.5-oz.) log refrigerated sugar cookie dough
- ✓ Assorted sanding sugar
- ✓ 1 bag marshmallows
- ✓ 1 (16-oz.) can vanilla frosting
- ✓ Green food coloring
  Pastel M&M's

Steps to Cook

1. Preheat oven to 350° and line two large baking sheets with parchment paper. Slice cookie dough into 1/4" rounds.
2. Place cookies about 1" apart on prepared baking sheets and bake according to package instructions. Let cool completely.
3. Pour each color of sanding sugar into a separate shallow bowl. Using scissors, cut marshmallows in half diagonally. Dip cut marshmallow ends in sanding sugar.
4. Add a few small drops of food coloring to frosting and stir until frosting is green. Spread green frosting over the top of each cookie, then place an M&M in the center.
5. For each cookie, arrange 5 marshmallows halves, sprinkle side-up, around the M&M to look like flower petals.

Teddy Bear Cookies

TIME TO PREPARE
15 minutes

COOK TIME
20 minutes

SERVING
12 Serving

PREPARED BY
Marie Austin

Ingredients

- ✓ Oatmeal cookie mix, plus ingredients called for on package
- ✓ Granulated ugar, for rolling
- ✓ Brown M&M's
- ✓ Mini chocolate chips

Steps to Cook

1. Preheat oven to 375° and line two large baking sheets with parchment paper. In a large bowl, prepare oatmeal cookie dough according to package instructions.

2. Shape cookie dough into six 1" balls for the bear head. Flatten bear heads with a glass. Shape smaller 1/2" balls for the ears and snouts. Place two balls on the top of each bear head to create ears. Roll the dough balls being used for snouts in sugar and place in the bottom center of the bear head. Carefully flatten the smaller balls.

3. Bake until golden, 8 to 10 minutes. While the bear cookies are still warm, place an M&M on the snout to make a nose and use two mini chocolate chips to make eyes.

4. Let cool completely.

Chocolate, Peanut Butter & Banana Bites

TIME TO PREPARE

10 minutes

COOK TIME

120 minutes

SERVING

6 Pencils

PREPARED BY

Cook Baker

Ingredients

- ✓ 1 c. semisweet chocolate chips
- ✓ 2/3 c. smooth peanut butter
- ✓ tsp. coconut oil
- ✓ bananas, sliced into 1/2"-thick rounds
- ✓ Flaky sea salt

Steps to Cook

1 Line a large, rimmed baking sheet with parchment paper.

2 In a medium bowl, heat chocolate in microwave in 30-second intervals until melted. Heat peanut butter for 15 seconds until runny.

3 In a medium bowl, mix chocolate and coconut oil until Merged.

4 Into a small baking cup, add a teaspoon scoop of chocolate. Top with a slice of banana, a teaspoon-size scoop of peanut butter, and another scoop of chocolate. Repeat until you have used all the banana slices. Top with a pinch of sea salt.

5 Place tray in freezer for 2 hours, or until frozen. Serve.

Funfetti Dump Cake

TIME TO PREPARE
10 minutes

COOK TIME
30 minutes

SERVING
6 People

PREPARED BY
Cook Baker

Ingredients

- ✓ 1 c. milk
- ✓ 1 box vanilla instant pudding mix
- ✓ 16 Golden Oreos (12 whole, 4 crushed)
- ✓ 1/2 c. white chocolate chips
- ✓ 1 box Funfetti cake mix
- ✓ 1 stick butter, thinly sliced
- ✓ 1/4 c. rainbow sprinkles

Steps to Cook

1. Preheat oven to 350°. In a bowl or glass measuring cup, Merge milk and vanilla pudding and Mix until thick, 2 minutes.
2. Spread pudding on the bottom of a 9"-x-13" baking dish. Top with a layer of 12 Golden Oreos and sprinkle with white chocolate chips.
3. Pour cake mix on top and use a fork to level out the mix, breaking up any clumps (especially around the corners).
4. Top with butter (spread all over) and sprinkle all over with crushed Oreos and sprinkles.
5. Bake until cake mix is completely baked through, 20 minutes. Let cool slightly before serving.

Strawberry Shortcake Lasagna

TIME TO PREPARE
25 minutes

COOK TIME
180 minutes

SERVING
12 Serving

PREPARED BY
Marie Austin

Ingredients

- ✓ 4 c. heavy cream
- ✓ 1/2 c. powdered sugar, plus more for dusting
- ✓ tsp. pure vanilla extract
- ✓ 1 1/2 boxes Nilla Wafers
- ✓ 1 lb. strawberries, thinly sliced

Steps to Cook

1. In a large bowl using a hand mixer, beat heavy cream, powdered sugar, and vanilla until medium peaks form.

2. Assemble lasagna: In a 9"-x-13" pan, spread a thin layer of whipped cream. Top with a layer of Nilla Wafers and spread a thick layer of whipped cream on top. Top with a layer of strawberries. Repeat two times, ending with strawberries. Sprinkle with crushed Nilla Wafers.

3. Refrigerate until Nilla Wafers are totally soft, 3 hours, or up to overnight.

4. Sprinkle with more powdered sugar, then slice and serve.

Unicorn Poke Cake

TIME TO PREPARE
30 minutes

COOK TIME
55 minutes

SERVING
6 Pencils

PREPARED BY
Cook Baker

Ingredients

- ✔ Cooking spray, for pan
- ✔ 1 box vanilla cake mix, plus ingredients called for on box
- ✔ Purple, teal, and pink food coloring
- ✔ 1 14-oz. can sweetened condensed milk

FOR THE FROSTING

- ✔ 1 c. butter, softened
- ✔ 1 1/2 c. powdered sugar
- ✔ 1 7-oz. jar marshmallow fluf
- ✔ 1 tsp. pure vanilla extract
- ✔ pinch of kosher salt
- ✔ 5 drops pink food coloring
- ✔ Sprinkles, for decorating

Steps to Cook

1. Preheat oven to 350º and grease a 9"-x-13" cake pan with cooking spray. Prepare cake batter according to package directions. Divide mixture into 3 bowls. In one bowl, add purple food coloring, in the second bowl add teal food coloring, and in the third bowl add pink food coloring.

2. Pour pink batter in prepared cake pan and spread to make an even layer. Top with purple batter and then teal batter.

3. Bake until a toothpick inserted in the center comes out clean, 24 to 25 minutes.

4. Let cake cool slightly, then use the bottom of a wooden spoon to poke holes all over cake.

5. Pour sweetened condensed milk all over poke holes.

6. Make frosting: In a large bowl using a hand mixer, beat together butter, powdered sugar, marshmallow fluff, vanilla, and salt. Add pink food coloring until you reach your desired color and beat until fully Merged.

7. Frost cake and decorate all over with sprinkles.

Ruffles Krispie Treats

TIME TO PREPARE
10 minutes

COOK TIME
40 minutes

SERVING
6 People

PREPARED BY
Cook Baker

Ingredients

- ✓ 1/4 c. butter
- ✓ 10 oz. bag mini marshmallows
- ✓ c. crushed Ruffles
- ✓ 1/2 tsp. Flaky sea salt
- ✓ 1/4 c. melted chocolate

Steps to Cook

1 Line an 8"-x-8" baking dish with parchment paper and spray with nonstick cooking spray.

2 In a medium saucepan over medium-low heat, melt butter. When butter has melted, turn off the heat and stir in mini marshmallows until completely melted. (If the marshmallows aren't melting, turn heat to low.)

3 Remove pot from heat and add crushed chips, then stir with a plastic spatula until well Merged. Immediately transfer mixture to prepared pan. Press down on mixture to make the bars more compact, then drizzle with melted chocolate.

4 Let treats cool to room temperature, about 30 minutes, before slicing.

Peanut Butter and Jelly Blondies

TIME TO PREPARE

15 minutes

COOK TIME

25 minutes

SERVING

12 Serving

PREPARED BY

Marie Austin

Ingredients

- ¾ cup (170 g) unsalted butter, at room temperature
- ½ cup (135 g) peanut butter
- 1 cup (212 g) dark brown sugar
- ½ cup (99 g) granulated sugar
- large eggs
- teaspoons pure vanilla extract
- 2¼ cups (271 g) all-purpose flour
- ¾ teaspoon baking powder
- ½ teaspoon baking soda
- ½ teaspoon fine sea sal
- ⅓ cup (103 g) seedless raspberry jam

Steps to Cook

1. Preheat the oven to 350°F. Grease a 9-by-13-inch baking pan with nonstick spray and line with parchment paper, allowing some excess paper to hang over the sides of the pan. Use scissors to cut the paper at the corners so it lies flush inside the pan.

2. In the bowl of an electric mixer fitted with the paddle attachment, cream the butter, peanut butter, brown sugar and sugar until light and fluffy, 4 to 5 minutes.

3. Add the eggs one at a time, mixing on medium speed until well Merged. Scrape the bowl well, then add the vanilla extract and mix to Merge.

4. Add the flour, baking powder, baking soda and salt; mix just until incorporated. Scrape the bowl well, then transfer to the prepared baking pan. Spread the batter into an even layer.

5. Transfer the jam to a disposable pastry bag (or a small zip-top plastic bag). Cut a ¼-inch opening from the end (or at one bottom corner of the zip-top bag).Squeeze the jam onto the surface of the blondies in swirly loops.

6. Transfer the pan to the oven and bake until the edges are golden brown and the surface appears set, 20 to 25 minutes. Cool completely in the pan.

7. Use the excess parchment paper to help pull the blondies out of the pan, then use a knife to cut into 12 even pieces.

Fruit Pizza

TIME TO PREPARE

15 minutes

COOK TIME

25 minutes

SERVING

12 Serving

PREPARED BY

Marie Austin

Ingredients

- ✓ BROWN SUGAR COOKIE CRUST:
- ✓ 1 1/2 cups all-purpose flour (plus extra for rolling)
- ✓ 1 teaspoon baking powder
- ✓ 1/4 teaspoon salt
- ✓ 1/2 cup (1 stick) unsalted butter, softened
- ✓ 1/2 cup packed light brown sugar
- ✓ 1 egg
- ✓ 1 teaspoon vanilla extract
- ✓ 1/2 teaspoon almond extract
- ✓ CREAM CHEESE FROSTING:
- ✓ 1 (8 ounce) package low-fat cream cheese
- ✓ 2–3 tablespoons maple syrup or honey (or 1 cup powdered sugar)
- ✓ 1 teaspoon vanilla extract
- ✓ pinch of fine sea salt
- ✓ TOPPINGS:
- ✓ fresh strawberries (blueberries, raspberries, blackberries, or any other fruit that sounds good!)
- o optional fresh honey, for drizzling

Steps to Cook

1. Heat oven to 350°F. Grease either a quarter sheet pan, a 9 x 13-inch baking dish, or a 12-inch round pizza pan with cooking spray.

2. In a medium bowl, Mix together the flour, baking powder and salt; set aside.

3. In a large mixing bowl either with a stand mixer (with the blade attachment) or hand mixer, beat the butter and sugar together on medium-speed until light and fluffy, about 2 minutes. Add the egg, vanilla and almond extract. Beat on medium speed until completely Merged, scraping down the sides partway through if needed. Add in the dry ingredients, and beat on low speed until just Merged. (Avoid over-mixing the dough.)

4. Press the dough evenly into the prepared pan/dish*. Use a fork to poke a few holes in the dough, to prevent it from bubbling up. Bake for 15-18 minutes, or until the dough is lightly golden. Transfer to a wire baking rack to let cool for 20 minutes.

5. Meanwhile, Mix together the frosting ingredients until Merged.

6. Spread the frosting out evenly on the baked cookie crust. Sprinkle with your favorite fruit, and drizzle with a bit of honey if desired. Slice, serve and enjoy!

Apple Dump Cake

TIME TO PREPARE
15 minutes

COOK TIME
45 minutes

SERVING
16 People

PREPARED BY
Marie Austin

Ingredients

- ✓ 5 medium apples (peeled, cored and sliced)
- ✓ 1 cup chopped nuts of your choice (lightly toasted)
- ✓ 4 teaspoons cinnamon (divided)
- ✓ 1 teaspoon freshly ground nutmeg
- ✓ 1/2 cup sugar
- ✓ 1 1/4 cup apple cider (or apple juice)
- ✓ 1 (18-ounce) box yellow cake mix
- ✓ 3/4 cup butter (melted)

Steps to Cook

1 Preheat oven to 375 F. Lightly grease a 9 x 13-inch pan.

2 In the pan, mix apples and nuts with 2 teaspoons cinnamon, nutmeg, and sugar.

3 Spread evenly in the pan and cover with apple cider.

4 Sprinkle dry cake mix over apple mixture. Sprinkle with remaining cinnamon.

5 Pour melted butter over top.

6 Bake for 45 minutes or until golden brown and bubbly.

7 Serve and enjoy!

Rice Crispy Treats

TIME TO PREPARE
10 minutes

COOK TIME
5 minutes

SERVING
6 People

PREPARED BY
Cook Baker

Ingredients

- ✓ 6 cups crispy rice cereal
- ✓ 3 tablespoons butter
- ✓ 4 cups mini marshmallows (or 10 ounces regular marshmallows)

Steps to Cook

1 Spray a heat-proof spatula and a 9 x 13 pan or jellyroll pan with cooking spray.

2 In a small saucepan, melt the butter and marshmallows over low heat, stirring frequently until the marshmallows are completely melted.

3 Pour over the crispy rice cereal.

4 Toss with the spatula to coat the cereal well.

5 Immediately transfer the rice crispy treats mixture to the prepared pan, and spread into an even layer with the spatula.

6 Let rice crispy treats cool completely before cutting into squares.

7 Serve and enjoy!

Blueberry Muffins

TIME TO PREPARE

12 minutes

COOK TIME

20 minutes

SERVING

12 People

PREPARED BY

Cook Baker

Ingredients

- ✓ 7 tablespoons unsalted butter (melted and cooled)
- 2/3 cup sugar
- ✓ large eggs
- ✓ 2/3 cup milk
- ✓ 1 1/2 teaspoons vanilla extract
- ✓ 1/4 teaspoon almond extract
- ✓ cups (9 ounces) all-purpose flour
- ✓ teaspoons baking powder
- ✓ 1/4 teaspoon baking soda
- ✓ 1/2 teaspoon salt
- ✓ 1 1/2 cups blueberries (fresh or frozen)
- ✓ 1 tablespoon sugar (mixed with 1/2 teaspoon cinnamon or 1/4 teaspoon vanilla extract)

Steps to Cook

1. Generously grease 12 muffin cups or spray with nonstick cooking spray or baking spray.
2. Heat the oven to 375 F.
3. In the bowl of an electric mixer, Merge the melted butter and sugar. Beat until smooth and well blended. Beat in the eggs, then slowly beat in the milk and vanilla and almond extracts.
4. In another bowl, Merge the flour with the baking powder, soda, and salt. Slowly beat into the first mixture until well blended.
5. With a spoon or rubber spatula, gently fold in the blueberries.
6. Fill the prepared muffin cups about 2/3 full. For uniform muffins, use a 1/4-cup scoop or measuring cup to measure the batter.
7. If desired, sprinkle with a mixture of 1 tablespoon of sugar and about 1/2 teaspoon of cinnamon. Or sprinkle a little vanilla sugar over the muffins.
8. Bake for 18 to 21 minutes, or until the muffins are lightly browned and a toothpick comes out clean when inserted into the center of a muffin.
9. Let cool in the pan on a rack for 10 minutes. Using a butter knife, carefully loosen the muffins from the muffin cups and remove to a rack to cool completely. Serve right away or freeze the cooled muffins on a rack or sheet pan then transfer to freezer bags and label. Thaw at room temperature or heat in the microwave or oven.
10. To reheat the frozen muffins, place an unwrapped muffin on a paper towel or paper plate and microwave on full power for about 25 to 30 seconds.
11. To reheat frozen muffins in the oven, wrap in foil and heat at 350 F for about 10 to 15 minutes.

Easy Vanilla Cupcakes

TIME TO PREPARE
20 minutes

COOK TIME
15 minutes

SERVING
12 People

PREPARED BY
Marie Austin

Ingredients

- ✓ 110g softened butter
- ✓ 110g golden caster sugar
- ✓ large eggs
- ✓ ½ tsp vanilla extract
- ✓ 110g self-raising flour
- ✓ For the buttercream
- ✓ 150g softened butter
- ✓ 300g icing sugar
- ✓ 1 tsp vanilla extract
- ✓ bsp milk
- ✓ food colouring paste of your choice (optional)

Steps to Cook

1 Heat oven to 180C/160C fan/gas 4 and fill a 12 cupcake tray with cases.

2 Using an electric Mix beat 110g softened butter and 110g golden caster sugar together until pale and fluffy then Mix in 2 large eggs, one at a time, scraping down the sides of the bowl after each addition.

3 Add ½ tsp vanilla extract, 110g self-raising flour and a pinch of salt, Mix until just Merged then spoon the mixture into the cupcake cases.

4 Bake for 15 mins until golden brown and a skewer inserted into the middle of each cake comes out clean. Leave to cool completely on a wire rack.

5 To make the buttercream, Mix 150g softened butter until super soft then add 300g icing sugar, 1 tsp vanilla extract and a pinch of salt.

6 Mix together until smooth (start off slowly to avoid an icing sugar cloud) then beat in 3 tbsp milk.

7 If wanting to colour, stir in the food colouring now. Spoon or pipe onto the cooled cupcakes.è

Cake Pops

TIME TO PREPARE

45 minutes

COOK TIME

20 minutes

SERVING

12 People

PREPARED BY

Cook Baker

Ingredients

- ✓ 100g butter
- ✓ 100g caster sugar
- ✓ ½ tsp vanilla extract
- ✓ eggs
- ✓ 100g self-raising flour
- ✓ For the buttercream
- ✓ 75g butter
- ✓ 150g icing sugar
- ✓ ½ tsp vanilla extract
- ✓ 1 tbsp milk
- ✓ 200g white chocolate, melted, to dip
- ✓ sprinkles, to dip

Steps to Cook

1   First make the cake. Heat oven to 190C/170C fan/gas 5. Grease and line the base of a 20cm sandwich tin. Place the butter, sugar and vanilla extract into a bowl and beat well to a creamy consistency. Slowly beat in the eggs, one by one, then fold in the flour and mix well. Tip into the cake tin and bake for about 20 mins until risen and golden brown. Set aside to cool completely.

2   While the cakes are cooling, make the buttercream. In a large bowl or the bowl of stand mixer, beat the butter and icing sugar together until smooth, add the vanilla extract and milk and beat again. Once the cake is cooled, crumble into large crumbs. Add the butter cream and stir together. Take chunks of the cake mixture and roll into balls, transferring each ball to a lined tray or plate, push a lollypop stick into each, then put into the fridge for an hour to set.

3   Melt the white chocolate in the microwave, blasting it and stirring at 10 seconds intervals until smooth. Tip the sprinkles into another bowl. Take each of the chilled cake pops and dip into the white chocolate, allowing it to drip off a little over the bowl. Dip into the sprinkles, then stand upright in a mug to dry at room temperature for an hour, or in the fridge for 30 mins.

Double-dipped Shortbread Cookies

TIME TO PREPARE

20 minutes

COOK TIME

30 minutes

SERVING

8 People

PREPARED BY

Marie Austin

Ingredients

- ✓ 200g salted butter , softened
- ✓ 100g icing sugar
- ✓ 1 tsp vanilla extract
- ✓ 250g plain flour
- ✓ 1 tbsp milk , plus extra if needed
- ✓ 50g white chocolate, chopped
- ✓ 50g milk chocolate , chopped

Steps to Cook

1   Heat the oven to 180C/160C fan/gas 4. Beat the butter with the icing sugar using an electric Mix until the mixture is light and fluffy. Beat in the vanilla and flour (the mixture will stiffen and look like crumble as the flour is added). Add the milk and keep beating until the mixture softens and sticks together (add some more milk if needed).

2   Scoop the dough into a piping bag fitted with a large star nozzle and pipe swirled rings onto a baking sheet lined with baking parchment. If the mixture is too stiff to pipe easily, you can roll the dough into balls and put them on the sheet instead. The cookies will spread as they cook so don't worry if there's a small gap in the centre of the piped swirls, but ensure there is enough space between each cookie so they don't stick together as they cook. Bake for 15 mins, or until lightly golden, then transfer to a wire rack to cool.

3   Put the white and milk chocolate in separate bowls and microwave each in 20-second bursts until melted. Dip the cookies into each chocolate, milk at one end and white on the other, then let any excess drip off before returning them to the rack to set. Will keep in an airtight tin for up to four days.

Unicorn Meringues

TIME TO PREPARE

20 minutes

COOK TIME

80 minutes

SERVING

12 People

PREPARED BY

Cook Baker

Ingredients

- ✓ large egg whites , at room temperature

- ✓ 100g caster sugar

- ✓ 100g icing sugar , sifted

- ✓ food colouring gels or pastes (we used pink, yellow, blue and green)

- ✓ small amount of white and black ready-to-roll fondant icing for the eyes and mouth

- ✓ You will also need

- ✓ 4cm round cutter or circle to drawn around

- ✓ 1 large piping bag fitted with a large open star nozzle (1cm)

- ✓ 4 small paintbrushes

Steps to Cook

1 Heat oven to 120C/100C fan/gas ½. Line 2 baking sheets with parchment. Using a 4cm round cutter as a guide, draw 22 circles on each piece of parchment in pencil. Turn the parchment over.

2 Whip up the egg whites in a stand mixer or with an electric hand Mix until they form stiff peaks. Gradually add the caster sugar in, a spoonful at a time, Mixing in completely between each addition. Repeat with the icing sugar until the mixture is glossy and stiff.

3 Put the piping bag nozzle down in a tall glass or jug. Roll down the top of the bag a little, over the rim, then paint a thin stripe of each coloured food gel from the nozzle all the way up to the top of the bag. Spoon in the meringue mixture.

4 Pipe swirls of meringue onto the trays using the circles as a guide. Bake for 20 mins then turn down to 100C/80C fan/gas ¼ and cook for a further hour, or until they are completely cooked through and sound hollow when tapped on the base. Leave to cool in the oven.

5 Mould small pieces of white and black fondant icing to create eyes and mouths. Stick these on the cooled meringues with a small dab of royal icing (if they don't stick by themselves).

Easy Birthday Cake

TIME TO PREPARE
20 minutes

COOK TIME
25 minutes

SERVING
8 People

PREPARED BY
Marie Austin

Ingredients

- ✓ 225g butter , at room temperature
- ✓ 225g golden caster sugar
- ✓ large eggs
- ✓ 225g self-raising flour
- ✓ tbsp whole milk
- ✓ 1 tsp vanilla extract
- ✓ tbsp cocoa powder
- ✓ For the pink icing
- ✓ 150g butter , very soft
- ✓ 300g icing sugar , sifted pink food colouring

Steps to Cook

1   Heat oven to 180C/160C fan/gas 4. Butter two 18cm loose-based cake tins and line the bases with baking parchment. Beat the butter and sugar in a mixer or by hand, then add the eggs, one at a time, mixing well after each. Fold in the flour, milk and vanilla extract until the mixture is smooth.

2   Divide the mixture between two bowls. Sift the cocoa powder into one of the bowls. Scrape the vanilla batter into one tin and the chocolate batter into the other and level the tops. Bake for 20-25 mins or until a skewer comes out clean. Cool for 5 mins, then transfer to a wire rack and cool completely.

3   To make the icing, beat the butter and add the icing sugar a little at a time, beating each lot in until you have a smooth, creamy icing. Add a little pink colour and beat it in (add more if you want a stronger colour). Sandwich the two cakes together with icing and spread the rest on top using a palette knife. Will keep in an airtight container for three days.

Peach Melba Pop Pies

TIME TO PREPARE
30 minutes

COOK TIME
20 minutes

SERVING
6 People

PREPARED BY
Marie Austin

Ingredients

- ✓ 200g raspberries
- ✓ 410g can peach slices in fruit juice , drained and chopped
- ✓ 1 tbsp cornflour
- ✓ 1 tbsp honey
- ✓ x 320g shortcrust pastry sheet
- ✓ 1 egg , beaten
- ✓ 150g icing sugar freeze-dried raspberries or sprinkles, optional

Steps to Cook

1 Set 6 plump raspberries aside and tip the rest into a bowl. Add the peaches and toss together. In a small bowl mix the cornflour and honey to make a paste, pour over the fruit and Merge.

2 Unroll the pastry sheets and use a pizza wheel to cut out 6 rectangles from each one. Turn a piece of pastry so the long side is nearest to you, and fold it in half like a book, to create a fold down the middle. Open the pastry out and spoon the fruit filling onto one side, leaving a border of about 1cm around the edge. Brush the beaten egg around the edges and fold the pastry again to encase the filling. Use a fork to seal the edges all the way around, then brush all over with more egg. Poke a few air holes in the top with the fork. Repeat with the remaining pastry and filling. Arrange the pop pies on a baking sheet lined with baking parchment and chill for at least 30 mins, or for up to 24 hrs. Alternatively freeze for up to 2 months.

3 Heat oven to 200C/180C fan/gas 6. Bake the pop pies for 20 mins, or until the pastry is golden and the filling is bubbling through the holes. Remove from the oven and cool for at least 20 mins. If cooking from frozen, bake for an extra 5 mins. Meanwhile crush the remaining raspberries until juicy and mix with the icing sugar to make a thick icing. Spread thinly over the pies and sprinkle with freeze dried raspberries or sprinkles, if you like. Eat warm, or cold, for breakfast or drizzle with cream or custard for dessert.

Sticky Upside-down Banana Cake

TIME TO PREPARE
15 minutes

COOK TIME
65 minutes

SERVING
12 People

PREPARED BY
Cook Baker

Ingredients

- ✓ 80g unsalted butter , plus extra for greasing
- ✓ 150g light muscovado sugar
- ✓ ½ tsp vanilla bean paste
- ✓ large bananas
- ✓ For the cake batter
- ✓ 240g plain flour
- ✓ ½ tsp baking powder
- ✓ 1 tsp cinnamon
- ✓ ½ tsp ground ginger
- ✓ 300g golden caster sugar
- ✓ 120g unsalted butter , very soft
- ✓ large eggs 150ml soured cream

Steps to Cook

1. Heat oven to 180C/160C fan/gas 4 and lightly grease a deep 23cm round cake tin, lining the base with baking parchment.

2. To make the topping, put the butter and sugar in a small saucepan and cook over a medium heat until melted and Merged. Add the vanilla and mix together. Pour the caramel into the cake tin and spread in an even layer. Cut the bananas in half lengthways and arrange on top of the caramel, cut-side down.

3. To make the batter, put all the ingredients in a large bowl with 1/4 tsp salt. Use an electric mixer to beat together on a low speed until the batter is smooth and evenly mixed. Pour the batter on top of the bananas and level out with a spatula. Bake in the oven for 55 mins-1 hr or until a skewer inserted in the middle comes out clean. If the cake begins to look too dark, cover with foil after 45 mins. Allow to cool in the tin for 10 mins before turning out onto a plate. Best served warm but also delicious at room temperature. Best eaten within 2 days.

Moon Cycle Cupcakes

TIME TO PREPARE
80 minutes

COOK TIME
25 minutes

SERVING
12 People

PREPARED BY
Marie Austin

Ingredients

- ✓ 175g softened unsalted butter
- ✓ 175g caster sugar
- ✓ large eggs
- ✓ 150g self-raising flour
- ✓ 50g cocoa powder
- ✓ tbsp icing sugar
- ✓ 100g blue ready-made fondant icing
- ✓ 100g black ready-made fondant icing
- ✓ 140g white fondant icing
- ✓ gold edible glitter (optional)

Steps to Cook

1 Line a 12-hole muffin tin with 12 dark brown or black muffin cases. Heat the oven to 180C/160C fan/gas 4. Put all the ingredients in a large bowl and using a hand-held electric Mix, beat for 2-3 minutes, until fluffy.

2 Divide the mixture between the muffin cases, then bake for 20 -25 minutes, until risen and springy to the touch – ask an adult to help you with this bit. When the cakes are cooked, take them out of the oven and transfer to a wire rack to cool completely – ask an adult to help you with this bit too. You will need 8 of the cakes to make a full cycle of the moon. If you need to, you can trim the tops of the cakes so that they are flat

3 Mix 3 tbsp of the icing sugar with enough water to make a spreadable paste and set aside. Knead the blue and black fondant icing together until the colours are almost blended together, leaving a few streaks of blue running through.

4 Dust a work surface with a little icing sugar and roll out the coloured icing so that it's large enough to cut out 12 x 7cm rounds. Spread a little smear of the icing sugar paste on top of each cake and stick an icing round on top.

5 Roll out the white icing to about 0.5cm thick. Using a small sharp knife, cut out 2 thin crescent shapes to make the waxing and waning crescent. Using a 7cm cutter, cut out 4 rounds. Cut one round in half to make the first and third quarter of the moon. Leave one round as it is to make the full moon and cut a small crescent away from the remaining 2 rounds, to make the waxing and waning gibbous moon. Using a little of the icing paste, stick each shape on to a cake. Leave one cake with nothing on – this will be the new moon. Use a star-shaped cutter to decorate the 4 cupcakes not included in the cycle with the leftover white icing.

6 Using a pastry brush, apply a tiny bit of water over the darker icing then sprinkle a little glitter over the top – the water helps it stick in place. Have fun arranging your cakes in a lunar cycle!

Lemon Curd & Blueberry Loaf Cake

TIME TO PREPARE	**SERVING**
20 minutes	8 People
COOK TIME	**PREPARED BY**
75 minutes	Marie Austin

Ingredients

- ✓ 175g softened butter , plus extra for greasing
- ✓ 500ml tub Greek yogurt (you need 100ml/3.5fl oz in the cake, the rest to serve)
- ✓ 300g jar good lemon curd (you need 2 tbsp in the cake, the rest to serve)
- ✓ eggs
- ✓ zest and juice 1 lemon , plus extra zest to serve, if you like
- ✓ 200g self-raising flour
- ✓ 175g golden caster sugar
- ✓ 200g punnet of blueberries (you need 85g/3oz in the cake, the rest to serve)
- ✓ 140g icing sugar edible flowers , such as purple or yellow primroses, to serve (optional)

Steps to Cook

1. Heat oven to 160C/140C fan/gas 3. Grease a 2lb loaf tin and line with a long strip of baking parchment. Put 100g yogurt, 2 tbsp lemon curd, the softened butter, eggs, lemon zest, flour and caster sugar into a large mixing bowl. Quickly mix with an electric Mix until the batter just comes together. Scrape half into the prepared tin. Weigh 85g blueberries from the punnet and sprinkle half into the tin, scrape the rest of the batter on top, then scatter the other half of the 85g berries on top. Bake for 1 hr 10 mins-1 hr 15 mins until golden, and a skewer poked into the centre comes out clean.

2. Cool in the tin, then carefully lift onto a serving plate to ice. Sift the icing sugar into a bowl and stir in enough lemon juice to make a thick, smooth icing. Spread over the top of the cake, then decorate with lemon zest and edible flowers, if you like. Serve in slices with extra lemon curd, Greek yogurt and blueberries.

Little Jam Tarts

TIME TO PREPARE

15 minutes

COOK TIME

15 minutes

SERVING

8 People

PREPARED BY

Cook Baker

Ingredients

- ✓ 500g sweet shortcrust pastry
- ✓ 20 tsp jam (we used apricot, blackcurrant and strawberry)

Steps to Cook

1. Roll out the shortcrust pastry on a lightly floured surface to just under the thickness of £1 coin. Stamp out 20 x 5cm circles using a pastry cutter and line 2 mini muffin tins (or make in 2 batches).

2. Prick with a fork and spoon 1 tsp jam into each (we used apricot, blackcurrant and strawberry). Stamp out shapes from the leftover pastry to decorate the tarts, if you like.

3. Bake at 200C/180C fan/gas 6 for 12-15 mins, until the pastry is golden.

Gingerbread man

TIME TO PREPARE

45 minutes

COOK TIME

15 minutes

SERVING

6 People

PREPARED BY

Marie Austin

Ingredients

- ✓ 140g unsalted butter
- ✓ 100g dark muscovado sugar
- ✓ 3 tbsp golden syrup
- ✓ 350g plain flour
- ✓ 1 tsp bicarbonate of soda
- ✓ 2 tsp ground ginger
- ✓ 1 tsp ground cinnamon
- pinch of cayenne pepper (optional)
- ✓ 2 balls stem ginger from a jar, chopped
- ✓ To decorate
- ✓ 50g icing sugar
- ✓ a few glacé cherries (we used undyed)
- ✓ 2 balls stem ginger

Steps to Cook

1. Heat oven to 200C/180C fan/gas 6. Line 2 baking sheets with baking parchment. Melt butter, sugar and syrup in a pan. Mix flour, soda, spices and a pinch of salt in a bowl. Stir in the butter mix and chopped ginger to make a stiff-ish dough.

2. Wait until cool enough to handle, then roll out dough to about 5mm thick. Stamp out gingerbread men, re-rolling and pressing the trimmings back together and rolling again. Lift onto baking sheets. Bake for 12 mins until golden. Cool 10 mins on the sheets, then lift onto cooling racks.

3. To decorate, mix icing sugar with a few drops of water until thick and smooth. Halve then slice cherries thinly to make smiles, and cut ginger into small squares. Spoon icing into a food bag, snip off the tiniest bit from one corner, then squeeze eyes and buttons, and a tiny smile onto 1 man at a time. Stick on a cherry smile and ginger buttons. Repeat; leave to set. Will keep up to 1 week in an airtight tin.

Peppermint Candy Biscuits

TIME TO PREPARE

25 minutes

COOK TIME

12 minutes

SERVING

8 People

PREPARED BY

Cook Baker

Ingredients

- ✓ 175g plain flour , plus a little extra for dusting
- ✓ 100g butter , cut into small cubes
- ✓ 85g caster sugar
- ✓ 1 egg yolk
- ✓ about 5 peppermint candy canes

Steps to Cook

1. Before you start, read the tips at the bottom of the recipe.

2. Tip the flour and butter into a bowl. Use your fingers to squash the lumps of butter into the flour, then rub together until the mixture resembles wet sand. Add the sugar and egg yolk and 1-2 tbsp cold water. Mix together with a blunt cutlery knife, then your hands, until it becomes a soft dough. (Or, get an adult to help you to do this in a food processor.) Wrap the dough in cling film and pop in the fridge for 20 mins to chill.

3. Heat oven to 200C/180C fan/gas 6. Line 2 baking trays with baking parchment. Put the candy canes in a resealable plastic bag, then wrap in a tea towel. Use a rolling pin to bash them to a chunky rubble. Set to one side.

4. Dust your work surface with a little flour, then use a rolling pin to roll out the dough. Cut out heart shapes with your big cookie cutter. Put them on the baking trays, spaced a little apart. Use your small cutter to cut out a little heart in the centre of each big heart. Re-roll your cuttings to make about 20 hearts in total.

5. Bake for 8 mins. Carefully remove the trays from the oven, then fill each small heart with a little of the crushed candy cane. Return to the oven for 4 mins more, until the biscuits are just starting to turn golden and the candy cane has melted.

a. Once out of the oven, quickly sprinkle the gooey centre of each heart with a little extra crushed candy cane. Leave to set and cool completely on the trays. Once cool, the biscuits will peel straight off the trays. Wrap them in pretty boxes to give as a gift.

Luscious Lemon Pudding

TIME TO PREPARE

15 minutes

COOK TIME

45 minutes

SERVING

4 People

PREPARED BY

Marie Austin

Ingredients

- ✓ 50g soft butter , plus extra for greasing
- ✓ 200g caster sugar
- ✓ 2 large lemons
- ✓ 3 large eggs
- ✓ 50g plain flour
- ✓ 300ml milk
- ✓ 200g strawberries
- ✓ 150g blueberries
- ✓ 2 tbsp blackcurrant cordial or 2 tbsp sugar
- ✓ icing sugar , for dusting

Steps to Cook

1. Butter an ovenproof dish and heat the oven to 180C/160C fan/ gas 4. Carefully weigh out the butter and sugar into a bowl.

2. Finely grate the zest from the lemons. For best results, grate, then turn the lemon a little and grate again, so you just take off the yellow skin rather than the pith below. Halve and squeeze the juice from the lemons – you need 100ml, so make up with a splash of water or more juice.

3. Separate the eggs (put the whites in a large, clean bowl), being careful not to get any yolk in with them. Whizz the butter, sugar and zest in a food processor until creamy. Add the juice, whizz again; then, with the motor still running, tip in the yolks, flour and milk to form a smooth batter.

4. Mix the egg whites, preferably with an electric hand Mix, until firm but not stiff. Pour in the lemon batter, then gently fold the 2 mixtures together with a large metal spoon, being light-handed so that you don't knock out all the air from the whites. Don't worry if it looks a bit lumpy.

5. Pour the mixture into the buttered dish, then put it in a roasting tin. Pour in a kettle of hot water into the tin so it is half-filled (this is called a bain marie). Ask an adult to help you with this bit. Bake for 35 mins until the top is set and there is a saucy lemon curd below. Use oven gloves to remove it from the oven.

6. While the pudding is baking, pull or cut the hulls (the green tops) from the strawberries. Halve or slice them if large. Put in a bowl with the blueberries, then spoon over the cordial or sugar and mix together. Remove the pudding from the tin, dust with icing sugar through a sieve and serve warm or cold, with the berries.

Sugared Scones

TIME TO PREPARE

20 minutes

COOK TIME

12 minutes

SERVING

8 People

PREPARED BY

Cook Baker

Ingredients

- ✓ 85g diced butter
- ✓ 350g self-raising flour
- ✓ ¼ tsp salt
- ✓ 1 ½ tsp bicarbonate of soda
- ✓ 4 tbsp caster sugar
- ✓ 200ml milk , warmed to room temperature, plus a splash extra
- ✓ crushed sugar cubes , to decorate

Steps to Cook

1. Heat oven to 200C/180C fan/gas 6. Whizz butter into flour. Tip into a bowl and stir in salt with bicarbonate of soda and sugar. Using a cutlery knife, quickly stir in milk – don't over-mix.

2. Tip out onto a lightly floured surface and turn over a couple of times to very gently bring together with your hands. Gently pat to about 1in thick, then stamp out rounds with a floured cutter. Pat together trimmings to stamp out more. Brush the tops with a splash more milk, then scatter with crushed sugar cubes. Bake on a baking sheet for 10-12 mins until risen and golden.

Very Chocolatey Cake

TIME TO PREPARE

35 minutes

COOK TIME

25 minutes

SERVING

6 People

PREPARED BY

Marie Austin

Ingredients

- ✓ 3 eggs
- ✓ 200g golden caster sugar
- ✓ 200g very soft butter
- ✓ 200g self-raising flour
- ✓ 1 tsp baking powder
- ✓ 3 tbsp cocoa powder
- ✓ 100g chocolate drops (milk, plain, white or a mix of all three)
- ✓ For the icing
- ✓ 300g soft butter
- ✓ 100g icing sugar
- ✓ 400g melted plain chocolate

Steps to Cook

1. Ask a grown-up to switch the oven on to 180C/160C fan/gas 4. Break the eggs into a small bowl and scoop out any bits of shell, then tip them into a large bowl.

2. Put the sugar and butter in a bowl, then sift over the flour, baking powder and cocoa.

3. Beat everything together using a wooden spoon or electric beaters, then stir in the chocolate drops.

4. Spoon half of the mixture into each tin and smooth the tops.

5. Ask a grown-up to bake the cakes for 20-25 mins or until risen and a skewer comes out clean. Cool in the tin for 5 mins, then turn out onto a rack.

6. Beat the butter and icing sugar, then fold in the chocolate. Spread over the middle, sandwich the cakes together, then dust with icing sugar.

Baked Lemon & Vanilla Rice Pudding

TIME TO PREPARE

5 minutes

COOK TIME

95 minutes

SERVING

6 People

PREPARED BY

Cook Baker

Ingredients

- ✓ 600ml milk
- ✓ 450ml single cream
- ✓ zest 1 unwaxed lemon
- ✓ 1 vanilla pod , split
- ✓ 25g caster sugar
- ✓ 100g short-grain pudding rice
- ✓ 25g butter , diced

Steps to Cook

1. Heat oven to 140C/120C fan/gas 1. Put the milk, cream, zest and vanilla pod in a saucepan. Gently bring to a simmer, then stir in the caster sugar and rice.

2. Transfer mixture to a shallow ovenproof dish and dot the butter on top. Bake for 30 mins, then stir well and cook for 1 hr more until the pudding is soft and creamy, and a golden skin has formed on top. The depth and type of dish you use will affect the cooking time, so if the pudding seems too loose, return to the oven and check every 10 mins or so. Once cooked, rest for 10 mins before serving.

Rocky Road Cookies

TIME TO PREPARE
15 minutes

COOK TIME
15 minutes

SERVING
8 People

PREPARED BY
Marie Austin

Ingredients

- ✓ 1 cup (226g) unsalted butter, at room temperature
- ✓ 1 cup (198g) granulated sugar
- ✓ ¾ cup (160g) light brown sugar
- ✓ 2 large (113g) eggs
- ✓ 2 teaspoons pure vanilla extract
- ✓ 2¼ cups (271g) all-purpose flour
- ✓ ⅔ cup (57g) cocoa powder
- ✓ ¾ teaspoon baking soda
- ✓ ½ teaspoon fine sea salt
- ✓ 1 cup (170g) chocolate chunks
- ✓ 1¼ cups (60g) mini marshmallows
- ✓ 1 cup (170g) chopped pecans

Steps to Cook

1. Preheat the oven to 350°F. Line two baking sheets with parchment paper.

2. In the bowl of an electric mixer fitted with the paddle attachment, cream the butter, sugar and brown sugar until light and fluffy, about 4 minutes.

3. Add the eggs one at a time, mixing until well Merged and scraping the bowl well after each addition. Add the vanilla and mix to Merge.

4. In a medium bowl, Mix the flour, cocoa powder, baking soda and salt to Merge. Add the flour mixture to the bowl of the mixer and mix to incorporate. Add the chocolate chunks, marshmallows and pecans, and mix until uniformly Merged.

5. Scoop the dough into ¼-cup-size balls onto the prepared baking sheets, staggering them to allow room to spread. Press the cookies flat (about 1 inch thick) with your fingers. Bake until the cookies are just set in the center, 12 to 15 minutes. Transfer to a cooling rack to cool completely.

Triple Cookie Skillet Pie

TIME TO PREPARE
20 minutes

COOK TIME
20 minutes

SERVING
6 People

PREPARED BY
Marie Austin

Ingredients

CHOCOLATE CHIP COOKIE DOUGH

- ✓ 4 tablespoons unsalted butter, melted
- ✓ ⅓ cup light brown sugar
- ✓ 3 tablespoons granulated sugar
- ✓ 1 large egg white
- ✓ ¾ teaspoon pure vanilla extract
- ✓ ⅔ cup all purpose flour
- ✓ ⅓ teaspoon baking soda
- ✓ Pinch fine sea salt
- ✓ ¾ cup chocolate chips

CHOCOLATE S'MORES COOKIE DOUGH

- ✓ 4 tablespoons unsalted butter, melted
- ✓ ½ cup light brown sugar
- ✓ 1 large egg white
- ✓ ¾ teaspoon pure vanilla extract
- ✓ ⅔ cup all-purpose flour
- ✓ 2 tablespoons cocoa powder
- ✓ ⅓ teaspoon baking soda
- ✓ Pinch fine sea salt
- ✓ ¾ cup chocolate chip
- ✓ 1 cup mini marshmallows

SNICKERDOODLE COOKIE DOUGH

- ✓ 4 tablespoons unsalted butter, melted
- ✓ ½ cup granulated sugar, plus 2 tablespoons
- ✓ 1 large egg white
- ✓ ¾ teaspoon vanilla extract
- ✓ ⅔ cup all purpose flour
- ✓ ⅓ teaspoon baking soda
- ✓ Pinch fine sea salt
- ✓ 1 cup pretzel M&Ms
- ✓ 1 teaspoon ground cinnamon

Steps to Cook

1. MAKE THE CHOCOLATE CHIP COOKIE DOUGH: In a medium bowl, stir together the melted butter, sugar and brown sugar. Add the egg white and vanilla, and mix well to Merge.

2. Add the flour, baking soda, and salt and mix to Merge. Mix in the chocolate chips.

3. MAKE THE CHOCOLATE S'MORES COOKIE DOUGH: In a medium bowl, stir together the melted butter and brown sugar. Add the egg white and vanilla, and mix well to Merge.

4. Add the flour, cocoa powder, baking soda, and salt and mix to Merge. Mix in the chocolate chips and marshmallows.

5. MAKE THE SNICKERDOODLE COOKIE DOUGH: In a medium bowl, stir together the melted butter and ½ cup sugar to Merge. Add the egg white and vanilla, and mix well to Merge.

6. Add the flour, baking soda and salt and mix to Merge. Mix in the M&Ms. In a small bowl, stir together the remaining 2 tablespoons sugar and cinnamon.

7. Lightly grease a 10-inch oven-safe skillet. Press each dough evenly into ⅓ of the skillet, leaving ½-inch of space between each type of cookie dough. Chill for 10 minutes. Preheat the oven to 350°F.

8. Sprinkle the cinnamon sugar over the snickerdoodle portion of the cookie. Bake the cookie until lightly golden brown, 17 to 20 minutes. Let cool at least 20 minutes before serving.

Lemon Bars

TIME TO PREPARE
15 minutes

COOK TIME
40 minutes

SERVING
8 People

PREPARED BY
Cook Baker

Ingredients

SHORTBREAD CRUST INGREDIENTS:

- ✓ 1 1/2 cups all-purpose flour
- ✓ 3/4 cup cold butter, diced
- ✓ 1/4 cup powdered sugar
- ✓ zest of 1 lemon

LEMON FILLING INGREDIENTS:

- ✓ 4 large eggs
- ✓ 1 cup powdered sugar
- ✓ 1/2 cup freshly-squeezed lemon juice
- ✓ 2 tablespoons all-purpose flour

Steps to Cook

1. Preheat oven to 350°F. Line an 8 x 8-inch baking pan with parchment paper; set aside.

2. Merge all of the crust ingredients in a food processor. Pulse until the mixture reaches a fine crumble consistency. You want the butter to be well Merged, but to stop before the mixture turns into a ball. (Alternately, you can Merge the crust ingredients together in a mixing bowl with a pastry cutter or a fork.)

3. Sprinkle the crust mixture evenly into the prepared pan. Then press the mixture down firmly to form an even layer.

4. Bake the crust for 20 minutes, or until it is lightly golden on top.

5. Meanwhile, Mix the lemon filling ingredients together in a medium mixing bowl until Merged. If your powdered sugar or flour are too chunky or there are lots of bubbles Mixed into the filling, feel free to just pour the filling through a fine-mesh strainer to get it nice and smooth before adding it to the crust. (But if there are a few little clumps, that's ok too!)

6. Once the crust is done baking, remove the pan from the oven and immediately pour the lemon filling on top of the hot crust. Return the pan to the oven and bake for 18-20 more minutes*, or until the lemon filling has set.

7. Remove the pan from the oven and transfer to a wire baking rack to cool until the bars reach room temperature. Then transfer to the refrigerator and let the bars chill for at least 2 hours.

8. Sprinkle the tops of the bars with extra powdered sugar*, if you would like, then slice and serve!

Banana Cake

TIME TO PREPARE
25 minutes

COOK TIME
30 minutes

SERVING
6 People

PREPARED BY
Cook Baker

Ingredients

Banana Cake

- ⅓ cup melted coconut oil or extra-virgin olive oil or high quality vegetable oil*
- ½ cup honey or maple syrup
- 2 large eggs
- 1 cup mashed ripe bananas (about 2 ½ medium or 2 large bananas)
- ¼ cup milk of choice or water
- 1 teaspoon baking powder
- ½ teaspoon baking soda
- 1 teaspoon vanilla extract
- ½ teaspoon salt
- ½ teaspoon ground cinnamon
- 1 cup white whole wheat flour or regular whole wheat flour
- ¾ cup whole wheat pastry flour or all-purpose flour
- Totally optional: ½ cup mix-ins like chopped walnuts or pecans, chocolate chips, raisins, chopped dried fruit, fresh banana slices…

Cream Cheese Frosting

- 8 ounces cream cheese, softened to room temperature
- 2 tablespoons unsalted butter, softened to room temperature
- 1 ¼ cups powdered sugar
- 1 teaspoon vanilla extract

Steps to Cook

1. To make the cake: Preheat the oven to 350 degrees Fahrenheit and grease a 9" square baker.

2. In a large bowl, beat the oil and honey together together with a Mix. Add the eggs and beat well, then Mix in the mashed bananas and milk. (If your coconut oil solidifies on contact with cold ingredients, simply let the bowl rest in a warm place for a few minutes, like on top of your stove, or warm it for 10 to 20 seconds in the microwave.)

3. Add the baking powder, baking soda, vanilla, salt and cinnamon, and Mix to blend. Add both flours, switch to a big spoon and stir just until Merged. Some lumps are ok! If you're adding any additional mix-ins, gently fold them in now.

4. Pour the batter into your greased baker. Bake for 30 to 34 minutes, or until a toothpick inserted into the center comes out clean. Place the cake pan on a cooling rack and let the cake cool completely before frosting.

5. To prepare the frosting: In a medium mixing bowl or the bowl of a stand mixer, Merge the softened cream cheese and butter. Using a hand mixer or a stand mixer (or your own strength), beat the cream cheese and butter together until fluffy.

6. Add the powdered sugar and vanilla and stir with a spoon until it is incorporated (or else powdered sugar will fly everywhere), then whip the frosting until it's nice and fluffy.

7. To assemble, spread frosting evenly over the top of the cake, then slice it and serve. This cake is best stored in the refrigerator for up to 4 days.

Holiday Pizzas

TIME TO PREPARE
30 minutes

COOK TIME
15 minutes

SERVING
4 People

PREPARED BY
Cook Baker

Ingredients

- ✓ For the dough
- ✓ 500g strong white bread flour , plus extra for dusting
- ✓ small pinch of sugar
- ✓ 7g sachet fast-action dried yeast
- ✓ tbsp olive oil , plus extra for greasing
- ✓ 300ml warm water
- ✓ For the sauce
- ✓ 1 garlic clove
- ✓ 400ml chunky passata
- ✓ 1 tbsp tomato purée
- ✓ 1 tsp dried oregano
- ✓ handful basil leaves , snipped
- ✓ small pinch of sugar
- ✓ 1 tsp red wine vinegar
- ✓ For the toppings
- ✓ ham, red peppers, black olives, salami, mozzarella , cherry tomatoes, cheddar, tuna, sweetcorn houmous and green salad, to serve

Steps to Cook

1   Mix a sticky dough. Put the flour, sugar and yeast in a bowl and get the child to make a hole in the middle. Measure 300ml water – that isn't cold and isn't hot but just right (like the little bear's porridge in Goldie Locks). Add the oil and water; point out that the two don't mix well. Stir with a wooden spoon until you have a sticky dough. Add a splash more water if needed.

2   Now you need to do something called kneading. Scatter a bit more flour over the surface and tip the dough onto it. You now want to 'stretch' the dough and bring it back into a ball shape. This will need to be done for about 10 mins. I usually give children a few minutes bashing the dough about, then take over to make sure that the dough is smooth and elastic enough.

3   Leave the dough to grow. Brush a clean bowl with a little olive oil, put the dough in it and cover with cling film. Leave it somewhere warm for it to grow until doubled in size. Now is a good time to tidy up and wipe down surfaces a little before you start again.

4   Make a tasty tomato sauce. Crush the garlic by using a garlic crusher or by grating it on the fine edge of a box grater. Tip into a bowl and mix with the other sauce ingredients. Stir well until everything is Merged, then set aside.

5   Roll out the dough. Heat oven to 220C/200C fan/gas 8. Show your child how the dough has grown, then divide into the amount of pizzas you want to make. Brush the baking trays with extra oil. Divide the dough and roll out, then lift onto the baking trays.

6   Spoon on the tomato sauce. You need to be a bit more careful with this task than you think. If the dough is thin, a child can easily tear it, so make sure that they use the back of the spoon to spread the sauce over. You can now freeze the pizzas – see tip, below

7   Build your own pizza. Put all the toppings out in different bowls and let the child 'build' their own pizza. Little ones will need to be handed the ingredients as they will try to just pile up as much as they can or not be able to scatter things evenly.

8   Get cooking. You can get older kids to carefully place the tray in the oven using oven gloves (see safety first, opposite). Bake pizzas for 12-15 mins until puffed up and golden around the edges, then carefully lift out of the oven. Leave to cool slightly, then slip onto a board or plate. Serve cut into pieces with houmous and a simple green salad.

Quick Pitta Pizzas

TIME TO PREPARE
10 minutes

COOK TIME
10 minutes

SERVING
2 People

PREPARED BY
Cook Baker

Ingredients

- ✓ wholewheat pitta breads
- ✓ tsp sun-dried tomato purée
- ✓ ripe plum tomatoes , diced
- ✓ 1 shallot , thinly sliced
- ✓ 85g chorizo , diced
- ✓ 50g mature cheddar , grated
- ✓ few basil leaves , if you like

Steps to Cook

1. Heat oven to 200C/180C fan/gas 6 and put a baking sheet inside to heat up. Spread each pitta with 1 tsp purée. Top with the tomatoes, shallot, chorizo and cheddar.

2. Place on the hot sheet and bake for 10 mins until the pittas are crisp, the cheese has melted and the chorizo has frazzled edges. Scatter with basil, if you like, and serve with a green salad.

Rainbow Pizzas

TIME TO PREPARE
20 minutes

COOK TIME
20 minutes

SERVING
4 People

PREPARED BY
Cook Baker

Ingredients

- ✓ 2 plain pizza bases
- ✓ 6 tbsp passata
- ✓ 400g mixed red and yellow tomatoes , sliced
- ✓ 75g sprouting broccoli , stems finely sliced
- ✓ 8 green olives , pitted and halved (optional)
- ✓ 150g mozzarella cherries (bocconcini)
- ✓ 2 tbsp fresh pesto
- ✓ handful fresh basil leaves, to serve

Steps to Cook

1   Heat the oven to 180C/160C fan/gas 4. Put each pizza base on a baking sheet and spread each with half of the passata. Arrange the tomatoes on the top in rings or wedges of colour and add the broccoli and the olives, if using. Squish the mozzarella cherries (bocconcini) a little before dotting them over the pizzas, then drizzle 1 tbsp pesto over each.

2   Bake for 15-20 mins or until the top is bubbling and just starting to brown a little. Scatter over the basil leaves before serving.

Pizza rolls

TIME TO PREPARE
15 minutes

COOK TIME
15 minutes

SERVING
6 People

PREPARED BY
Cook Baker

Ingredients

- ✓ 6 crusty bread rolls
- ✓ 2 tbsp tomato purée
- ✓ 6 slices ham
- ✓ 3 tomatoes , sliced
- ✓ 2 balls mozzarella , sliced (we used Sainsbury's Basics)
- ✓ 2 tsp dried oregano
- ✓ 6 black olives (optional)

Steps to Cook

1. Heat oven to 180C/160C fan/gas 4. Cut the tops off the rolls and scoop out the insides. Spread the rolls with tomato purée, then fill with ham, tomatoes and finally the mozzarella. Scatter with dried oregano and top each with an olive, if you like.

2. Place the rolls on a baking tray and bake for 15 mins until the rolls are crusty brown and the cheese is bubbling. Leave to rest for a min, then serve hot with a side salad.

Pizza With Homemade Sauce

TIME TO PREPARE
30 minutes

COOK TIME
20 minutes

SERVING
4 People

PREPARED BY
Cook Baker

Ingredients

- ✓ 300g strong white bread flour , plus extra for dusting
- ✓ 1 tsp instant yeast
- ✓ 1 tbsp olive oil
- ✓ For the tomato sauce
- ✓ 1 tbsp olive oil , plus a drizzle
- ✓ 2 garlic cloves , crushed
- ✓ 200ml passata
- ✓ For the topping
- ✓ 8 mozzarella pearls , halved
- ✓ small bunch fresh basil

Steps to Cook

1 Tip the flour into a bowl, then stir in the yeast and 1 tsp salt. Make a well in the centre and pour in 200ml warm water (make sure it's not too hot) along with the oil. Stir together with a wooden spoon until you have a soft, fairly wet dough.

2 Tip the dough out onto a lightly floured surface and knead for 5 mins until smooth. Cover with a tea towel and set aside for an hour or so or until the dough has puffed up and doubled in size. You can also leave the rough, unkneaded dough in the bowl, cover with a tea towel and leave in the fridge overnight and the dough will continue to prove on its own

3 Meanwhile, make the tomato sauce. Put the oil in a small pan and fry the garlic briefly (don't let it brown), then add the passata and simmer everything until the sauce thickens a little. Leave to cool

4 Once the dough has risen, knead it quickly in the bowl to knock it back, then tip out onto a lightly floured surface and cut into two balls. Roll out each ball into a large teardrop that is very thin and about 25cm across (teardrop shapes fit baking sheets more easily than rounds).

5 Heat oven to 240C/220C fan/ gas 9 with a large baking sheet inside. Lift one of the bases onto another floured baking sheet. Smooth the sauce over the base with the back of a spoon, scatter over half the mozzarella, drizzle with olive oil and season. Put the pizza, still on its baking sheet, on top of the hot sheet in the oven and bake for 8-10 mins until crisp.

Tuna, Olive & Rocket Pizzas

TIME TO PREPARE
15 minutes

COOK TIME
12 minutes

SERVING
2 People

PREPARED BY
Cook Baker

Ingredients

- ✓ 145g pack pizza base mix (or same weight of bread mix)
- ✓ 2 tbsp tomato purée
- ✓ 185g can tuna in oil, drained, oil reserved
- ✓ plain flour , for dusting
- ✓ 1 tbsp caper
- ✓ 125g pack value mozzarella
- ✓ 10 pitted black kalamata olives
- ✓ 1 small red onion , halved and thinly sliced
- ✓ small handful rocket

Steps to Cook

1 Heat oven to 240C/220C fan/gas 9. Tip the pizza mix into a bowl and make up following pack instructions. Cover the bowl with a cloth and leave for a few mins.

2 Meanwhile, mix the tomato purée with 4 tbsp water, 1 tbsp oil from the tuna and some seasoning.

3 Knead the dough for a few mins on a floured surface, then halve and put each piece, spaced apart, on a large oiled baking tray. Press with an oiled hand to make thin flat pizzas – they don't have to be perfectly round.

4 Spread with the tomato purée mixture, then top with the tuna, capers, cheese and olives. Bake for 10-12 mins. Serve scattered with the onion and rocket.

Mozzarella, Ham & Pesto Pizzas

TIME TO PREPARE
10 minutes

COOK TIME
10 minutes

SERVING
2 People

PREPARED BY
Cook Baker

Ingredients

- ✓ 4 mini pitta breads
- ✓ 150g pack mozzarella
- ✓ 4 tsp pesto
- ✓ 85g smoked wafer thin ham

Steps to Cook

1. Turn the grill to high, put the pittas on the grill rack and heat for about a minute while you slice the mozzarella into five.

2. Turn the pittas over and spread each one with 1 tsp pesto, then top with a mozzarella slice. Pile the ham on top, so it looks quite ruffled, then tear the final mozzarella slice into four, put it on top of the ham and grind over black pepper. Return to the grill for 3-4 minutes more until melted and starting to turn golden.

Cheese & Bacon Scone Pizza

TIME TO PREPARE
15 minutes

COOK TIME
15 minutes

SERVING
4 People

PREPARED BY
Cook Baker

Ingredients

- ✓ For the scone base
- ✓ 250g plain flour
- ✓ 1 tsp salt
- ✓ 2 tsp baking powder
- ✓ 50g butter , chopped
- ✓ 2 eggs
- ✓ 3 tbsp milk
- ✓ For the cheesy topping
- ✓ 1 tbsp olive oil
- ✓ 1 green pepper , quartered, deseeded and thinly sliced
- ✓ 4 rashers streaky bacon , chopped
- ✓ 5 spring onions , thinly sliced (the white and green parts)
- ✓ 2 tbsp tomato ketchup mixed with 2 tbsp tomato purée
- ✓ about 6-8 cherry tomatoes , halved
- ✓ 85g mature cheddar , grated

Steps to Cook

1. Heat oven to 220C/fan 200C/gas 7. Mix the flour, salt and baking powder in a bowl, then rub in the butter until it disappears. Mix the eggs and milk together, then stir into the dry ingredients to make a soft dough. Shape into a round on a lightly floured surface, lift onto a non-stick baking tray, then press out to a circle about 24cm across to make the pizza base.

2. Heat the oil in a frying pan, then stir-fry the pepper and bacon until the pepper is soft. Take off the heat, then stir in the spring onion.

3. Spread the ketchup over the pizza base, then evenly tip over the pepper and bacon mixture. Scatter over the tomatoes, followed by the cheese. Bake for 15 mins until golden. Serve with a salad or coleslaw.

Tuna Melt Pizza Baguettes

TIME TO PREPARE
10 minutes

COOK TIME
20 minutes

SERVING
4 People

PREPARED BY
Cook Baker

Ingredients

- ✓ 2 part-baked baguettes
- ✓ 1 red pepper , diced
- ✓ 1 green pepper , diced
- ✓ 198g can sweetcorn , drained
- ✓ 225g jar tuna
- ✓ 100g cheddar , grated
- ✓ 1 tbsp tomato purée

Steps to Cook

1 Heat oven to 190C/170C fan/gas 5. Halve the 2 part-baked baguettes lengthways and cook directly on the oven shelf for 8 mins. Meanwhile mix the diced peppers, sweetcorn, tuna, and 75g of the grated cheddar.

2 Transfer the baguettes to a baking tray, spread each with 1 tbsp tomato purée, divide the tuna mix over, then sprinkle with the remaining grated cheddar. Bake for 12 mins until melting and golden.

Chorizo and Spanish black Olive Pizza

TIME TO PREPARE
75 minutes

COOK TIME
15 minutes

SERVING
2 People

PREPARED BY
Cook Baker

Ingredients

- ✓ 230g strong white flour
- ✓ 1 teaspoon salt
- ✓ 1 teaspoon dried yeast
- ✓ ½ teaspoon caster sugar
- ✓ 2 tablespoons olive oil
- ✓ 125ml warm water
- ✓ dusting of flour
- ✓ 4 tablespoons tomato sauce
- ✓ 50g semi-cured Manchego cheese, shaved
- ✓ 100g fresh chorizo, cubed
- ✓ 12 Spanish black olives, pitted
- ✓ 1 pinch of sea salt and freshly ground black pepper
- ✓ 1 teaspoon dried oregano

Steps to Cook

1   The Base: Sift the flour into a mixing bowl. Add the salt, the yeast and then the sugar. Mix together and then make a well in the middle of the mixture.

2   Mix 1 tablespoon of the olive oil and the water together and add it into the flour mixture. Mix well with your fingers; you will finish with a soft ball and the bowl will be clean when you have finished mixing. Place the dough onto a floured work surface and knead it well for approximately 4 minutes.

3   Transfer the dough to an oily bowl and rub the surface of the dough with a little more oil, cover with a damp cloth and keep in a warm place to rise for about 1 hour – the dough should double in size.

4   Preheat the oven to 220 C / gas 7.

5   Place the dough on a floured work surface and knead for 3 more minutes. With your hands, stretch the dough to make the shape and thickness you want. Brush with olive oil and place the pizza base on a non-stick baking tray.

6   Topping: Now we can start topping the Spanish pizza. First place the tomato sauce on the base and spread well. Add the cheese, chorizo cubes and olives and season with salt and pepper and oregano.

7   Place the pizza in the oven and bake for approximately 15 minutes or until the edges are turning golden.

8   Serve with a green salad.

Smoked Aubergine and Burrata Pizza

TIME TO PREPARE
45 minutes

COOK TIME
20 minutes

SERVING
4 People

PREPARED BY
Cook Baker

Ingredients

For the dough
- ✓ 50ml warm water
- ✓ 5g dried yeast
- ✓ 1 teaspoon sugar
- ✓ 1kg strong white flour
- ✓ 550ml water
- ✓ 30g salt

For the smoked aubergine topping
- ✓ 1 aubergine
- ✓ 1 red pepper
- ✓ sea salt and pepper to taste
- ✓ cayenne pepper
- ✓ 2 tablespoons extra virgin olive oil

For the tomato sauce
- ✓ 1 tin chopped tomatoes
- ✓ 1 clove garlic, crushed
- ✓ fresh basil to taste
- ✓ chilli flakes to taste
- ✓ 1 pinch salt
- ✓ 1 pinch sugar
- ✓ Extras
- ✓ cubed mozzarella cheese
- ✓ burrata cheese, to taste
- ✓ grated Pecorino Romano cheese, to taste
- ✓ fresh rocket leaves

Steps to Cook

1. Pizza dough:
2. Mix 50ml warm water with yeast and sugar. Let stand till foamy.
3. Put the flour in an adequate sized bowl, make a well in the middle and add remaining water, plus the yeast mixture. Mix by hand until you form a lovely dough ball using any excess flour to dry off hands if they get sticky. (Ingredients can also go into a food processor; you'll know when it's ready because the dough ball rolls to one side.)
4. Cover the dough ball in a bowl with cling film and leave to rise in a dark room until double the size.
5. On a flat surface divide into 6 dough balls about 270g each in weight. Once again leave to rise on a baking tray until double in size.
6. Dust surface, take a ball and begin to push it open with your hands until around 12 inches in diameter, using a rolling pin if required. Once again leave to rest for around 10 minutes then it's time to add the toppings.
7. Aubergine topping:
8. Take 1 clean aubergine and 1 red pepper and grill so that the skins blister and slightly blacken which is what gives the smoked flavour. Make sure you watch these because they can easily burn, so continue to rotate.
9. When they are soft and juicy to the touch (aubergine will take a bit longer) remove from the grill and leave to cool enough so that you can peel the skins off by hand.
10. Once peeled, chop or pulse aubergine and pepper together to a chunky texture. Then season to taste with sea salt, ground black pepper and cayenne pepper. Add 2 tablespoons of good extra virgin olive oil.
11. Tomato sauce:
12. Pulse tinned tomatoes to a smooth but chunky texture. Add salt, pepper, chilli, garlic, fresh basil a pinch of sugar and a pinch of salt.
13. To finish:
14. Heat up oven to maximum temperature.
15. Add the tomato sauce to the opened pizza which is resting happily on a baking sheet; use the base of a large spoon to spread evenly, spread the smoked aubergine mixture in a similar way, 50g of smoked aubergine dip is ample. Add mozzarella, sprinkle evenly over each pizza.
16. Bake each pizza until golden. When the pizza comes out add the hand broken burrata, fresh basil and Pecorino too if you like, and fresh rocket is also good.

Homemade Pepperoni Pizza

⏱ **TIME TO PREPARE**
30 minutes

🍲 **COOK TIME**
20 minutes

🍴 **SERVING**
2 People

⏻ **PREPARED BY**
Cook Baker

Ingredients

- ✓ 1 tablespoon dried yeast
- ✓ 1 pinch of salt
- ✓ 140ml warm water
- ✓ 180g strong plain flour
- ✓ 1 tablespoon olive oil
- ✓ 1 tin chopped tomatoes
- ✓ 2 tablespoons tomato puree
- ✓ 1 onion, chopped
- ✓ 2 cloves of garlic, chopped thinly
- ✓ grated cheese or mozarella
- ✓ 1 packet pepperoni slices
- ✓ 1 tablespoon dried basil

Steps to Cook

Pizza base:

Mix salt and yeast together in a jug with the water. Place flour in a bowl, make a well in the centre and add the water mixture along with the oil. Use a wooden spoon to mix everything to create a wet dough. Put on floured surface and knead for 5 minutes.

Place in greased bowl and cover with tea towel. Leave at room temperature to rise for 30 minutes (should double in size).

Round into a pizza base and stab with fork several times.

Pizza topping:

Spread tomato puree over the base. Add chopped tomatoes on top then add onion and garlic. Sprinkle over cheese and arrange pepperoni. Season with salt and pepper and sprinkle on basil.

Place on oiled baking tray. Cook at 200 C / Gas 6 for 20 minutes.

Onion and Red Pepper Pizza

TIME TO PREPARE
40 minutes

COOK TIME
20 minutes

SERVING
4 People

PREPARED BY
Cook Baker

Ingredients

- ✓ 250g plain flour
- ✓ 1 pinch salt
- ✓ 2 teaspoons dried active baking yeast
- ✓ 150ml water
- ✓ 6 tablespoons olive oil
- ✓ 1 red pepper
- ✓ 3 onions, sliced
- ✓ 1 tin passata
- ✓ 150g grated Gruyère cheese
- ✓ 2 pinches herbes de Provence

Steps to Cook

1. Mix together the flour, salt and dried active baking yeast. Stir in the warm water and 3 tablespoons of the olive oil to form a soft dough. Turn the dough out onto a lightly floured board, and knead, until smooth and elastic, about 10 minutes.

2. Cover the dough and let rise in a warm place until doubled in volume, about 35 minutes.

3. Preheat the oven to 220 C / Gas 7. Oil a pizza tray.

4. Roast the red pepper for 10 minutes in the preheated oven. Peel, seed and slice the pepper into thin slices. Meanwhile, heat the remaining 3 tablespoons olive oil over medium heat in a frying pan, and cook and stir the onions until golden, about 5 minutes.

5. Roll out the pizza base on a lightly floured board, and transfer the base to the prepared pizza tray. Spread the pizza base with passata. Add the onions evenly over the top and sprinkle with the grated Gruyère cheese. Arrange the pepper slices over the cheese and sprinkle with the herbes de Provence.

6. Bake in the preheated oven until the pizza base is golden and the cheese is bubbly, about 10 minutes.

Bacon, Asparagus and Goat Cheese Pizza

TIME TO PREPARE
15 minutes

COOK TIME
25 minutes

SERVING
8 People

PREPARED BY
Cook Baker

Ingredients

- ✓ 5 bacon rashers, cut into 2cm pieces
- ✓ 1 unbaked pizza base
- ✓ 200g grated mozzarella cheese
- ✓ 150g chopped fresh asparagus
- ✓ 125g halved cherry tomatoes
- ✓ 300g goat cheese
- ✓ 1 teaspoon red chilli flakes
- ✓ freshly ground black pepper to taste

Steps to Cook

1 Preheat the oven to 190 C / Gas mark 5.

2 Place bacon in a frying pan over medium-high heat. Cook for a few minutes, but do not cook until crisp. Remove to kitchen roll and set aside.

3 Place the pizza base on a pizza tin or large baking tray. Top with mozzarella cheese, bacon pieces, asparagus and tomatoes. Dot with goat cheese, then season with red chilli flakes and black pepper.

4 Bake for 15 to 20 minutes in the preheated oven, until the crust is golden brown underneath when you lift it up to take a peek. Let cool for about 3 to 5 minutes before slicing and serving.

Pizza alla Napoletana

TIME TO PREPARE
135 minutes

COOK TIME
25 minutes

SERVING
4 People

PREPARED BY
Cook Baker

Ingredients

- 340 g (12 oz) strong white (bread) flour
- ½ tsp salt
- 1 sachet easy-blend dried yeast, about 7 g
- 200 ml (7 fl oz) tepid water
- 2 tbsp extra virgin olive oil
- Napoletana topping
- 2 tbsp extra virgin olive oil
- 1 small onion, finely chopped
- 2 garlic cloves, crushed
- 2 cans chopped tomatoes, about 400 g each
- ½ tsp caster sugar
- small handful of fresh basil leaves, torn into pieces
- 150 g (5½ oz) mozzarella cheese, thinly sliced
- 8 anchovy fillets, halved lengthways
- 8 black olives, stoned and halved
- salt and pepper

Steps to Cook

1. Put the flour into a bowl and stir in the salt and yeast. Make a well in the centre and add the water and olive oil. Mix with a round-bladed knife until the mixture forms a soft dough, adding a little more water if it feels too dry.

2. Turn the dough out onto a lightly floured surface and knead for about 10 minutes or until smooth and elastic. Place the dough in a large, lightly greased bowl, cover with cling film and leave to rise in a warm place for 1–1 1/2 hours or until double 1/2 in size.

3. Meanwhile, make the topping. Heat the olive oil in a saucepan, add the onion and garlic, and cook gently, stirring, for 3 minutes or until softened. Add the tomatoes with their juice, the sugar, and salt and pepper to taste, and bring to the boil. Leave the mixture to bubble, stirring frequently, until reduced by about half to make a thick sauce. Remove from the heat and leave to cool.

4. Turn out the risen dough onto the lightly floured surface and knock it back, then knead very lightly. Roll or press out to a round about 30 cm (12 in) in diameter and transfer to a greased baking sheet.

5. Stir the basil into the tomato sauce. Spread the sauce over the pizza base to within 1 cm (1/2 in) of the edge. Arrange the mozzarella, anchovies and olives over the top, then leave the pizza in a warm place for about 15 minutes. Meanwhile, preheat the oven to 220ºC (425ºF, gas mark 7).

6. Bake the pizza for 20–25 minutes or until the crust has risen and is golden and the cheese has melted. Cut into wedges and serve warm.

7. Each slice provides

8. B6, B12, calcium * A, B1, C, E, niacin, selenium * B2, folate, iron, zinc

9. Some more ideas

10. To make roasted vegetable pizza, cut 2 small red onions into wedges; cut 1 red and 1 yellow pepper into chunks; and thinly slice ½ small aubergine (about 150 g/5½ oz). Toss the vegetables with 4 tbsp extra virgin olive oil in a roasting tin, then roast in an oven preheated to 200ºC (400ºF, gas mark 6) for 30 minutes or until soft and just beginning to char. Arrange the vegetables on the tomato sauce in place of the mozzarella and anchovies, and scatter over the olives. After baking, sprinkle with 30 g (1 oz) Parmesan cheese, cut into shavings. * To make spinach, mushroom and chorizo pizza, put 200 g (7 oz) baby spinach leaves in a saucepan, cover and cook for 1–2 minutes or until just wilted; drain well. Fry 200 g (7 oz) sliced chestnut mushrooms in 15 g (½ oz) butter until their liquid has evaporated and they are just starting to colour. Arrange the spinach and mushrooms on the tomato sauce in place of the mozzarella, anchovies and olives. Scatter over 30 g (1 oz) thinly sliced chorizo sausage and 2 tbsp pine nuts, then rise and bake.

Porcini Pizza

TIME TO PREPARE
20 minutes

COOK TIME
2 minutes

SERVING
12 People

PREPARED BY
Cook Baker

Ingredients

- ✓ 1.13kg bread flour
- ✓ 30g salt
- ✓ 1 tablespoon honey
- ✓ 600ml warm water
- ✓ 1 (7g) sachet dried active baking yeast
- ✓ 3 tablespoons olive oil
- ✓ 1 clove garlic, finely chopped
- ✓ 225g rehydrated porcini mushrooms
- ✓ salt and pepper to taste
- ✓ 2 tablespoons dry polenta
- ✓ 110g grated Fontina cheese
- ✓ 40g grated Parmesan cheese
- ✓ 2 tablespoons chopped fresh parsley

Steps to Cook

1. Merge the flour, salt, honey and warm water in an electric mixer with a dough hook. Mix on low for 2 minutes. Add the yeast and let mix for another 6 minutes on medium speed. Add the oil and let mix for another 2 minutes. The dough should be fairly tough. Portion into 175g balls. The rounder the balls, the rounder the pizza in the end. Place the balls in a warm place covered with a moist towel and let double in size.

2. Preheat oven to 230 C / Gas 8 and place a pizza stone in the oven to preheat with the oven. Be sure to put the pizza stone in when the oven is cold to help it preheat.

3. Heat the olive oil in a large frying pan over medium heat. Stir in the garlic and saute for 30 seconds. Then add the mushrooms and saute for about 2 more minutes. Season with salt and pepper to taste.

4. On a lightly floured surface, pat or roll out the pizza dough to about a 5mm thickness. Place on a wooden plank dusted with polenta and brush the base lightly with olive oil. Sprinkle the Fontina and Parmesan cheeses over the base, followed by the sauteed mushrooms. Carefully transfer the pizza to the pizza stone.

5. Bake at 230 C / Gas 8 for about 10 to 15 minutes or until base is golden brown and cheese is melted and bubbly. Garnish with the parsley.

Hedgehog Rolls

TIME TO PREPARE
20 minutes

COOK TIME
15 minutes

SERVING
5 People

PREPARED BY
Cook Baker

Ingredients

- ✓ 500g pack brown bread mix
- ✓ 25g butter
- ✓ plain flour , for dusting
- ✓ raisins
- ✓ 6 flaked almonds

Steps to Cook

1 Make the bread mixture with the butter following pack instructions. It's easiest to use a stand mixer but not difficult to do by hand. Leave the dough to rest for 5 mins, then knead for 5 mins.

2 Cut the dough into six pieces. Dust the surface with a little flour and shape each piece into a ball by rolling it between your hand. Now make it hedgehog-shaped by pulling one side out a little and squeezing it gently into a snout. Be quite firm or it will bounce back.

3 Put the hedgehogs on a baking sheet, cover with a damp tea towel and leave to rise for 1 hr.

4 Heat oven to 200C/180C fan/gas 6. Using kitchen scissors (supervise younger children), carefully snip into the dough to make the spikes on the backs of the hedgehogs. Press raisins in for the eyes and push a flaked almond into the end of each snout.

5 Bake for 15 mins or until the rolls are risen and golden. Will keep for two days in an airtight container.

Easy Bread

TIME TO PREPARE
15 minutes

COOK TIME
35 minutes

SERVING
8 People

PREPARED BY
Cook Baker

Ingredients

- ✓ 500g granary, strong wholewheat or white bread flour (I used granary)
- ✓ 7g sachet fast-action dried yeast
- ✓ 1 tsp salt
- ✓ 2 tbsp olive oil
- ✓ 1 tbsp clear honey

Steps to Cook

1 Tip the flour, yeast and salt into a large bowl and mix together with your hands. Stir 300ml hand-hot water with the oil and honey, then stir into the dry ingredients to make a soft dough.

2 Turn the dough out onto a lightly floured surface and knead for 5 mins, until the dough no longer feels sticky, sprinkling with a little more flour if you need it

3 Oil a 900g loaf tin and put the dough in the tin, pressing it in evenly. Put in a large plastic food bag and leave to rise for 1 hr, until the dough has risen to fill the tin and it no longer springs back when you press it with your finger.

4 Heat oven to 200C/fan 180C/gas 6. Make several slashes across the top of the loaf with a sharp knife, then bake for 30-35 mins until the loaf is risen and golden. Tip it out onto a cooling rack and tap the base of the bread to check it is cooked. It should sound hollow. Leave to cool.

Flowerpot Bread

TIME TO PREPARE
25 minutes

COOK TIME
25 minutes

SERVING
5 People

PREPARED BY
Cook Baker

Ingredients

- ✓ 500g granary, strong, wholemeal or white bread flour
- ✓ 7g sachet fast-action dried yeast
- ✓ 1 tsp salt
- ✓ 2 tbsp olive oil , plus extra for the flowerpots
- ✓ 1 tbsp clear honey
- ✓ a little milk or oil, for brushing

  Plus any of these toppings

- ✓ 1 tbsp pumpkin, sunflower, sesame or poppy seed
- ✓ 4 tbsp grated cheddar or crumbled feta cheese
- ✓ 1 tbsp chopped rosemary, thyme, oregano, chives or basil
- ✓ 1 tbsp chopped olive or sundried tomatoes
- ✓ ½ tsp chilli flakes

  You will also need

- ✓ 5 small, clean clay flowerpots (see tip below), baking parchment and cling film

Steps to Cook

1. Tip the flour, yeast and salt into a large bowl. Pour in 300ml warm water, the olive oil and honey. Mix with a wooden spoon until the mixture clumps together, then tip out onto a work surface. Use your hands to stretch and knead the dough for about 10 mins, or until it's smooth and springy. Add a little extra flour if the dough feels too sticky.

2. Brush the flowerpots with oil and line the sides with baking parchment. Divide the dough into 5 pieces and shape into smooth balls. Place one ball of dough into each flowerpot and cover with cling film. Leave in a warm place for 1 hr to rise.

3. Heat oven to 200C/180C fan/gas 6. When the dough has doubled in size, remove the cling film from the pots and gently brush with a little milk or oil. Sprinkle with your choice of topping.

4. Place the pots on a baking tray in the oven and cook for 20-25 mins until risen and golden. The pots will be very hot, so be careful when removing from the oven. Leave to cool for 10 mins before turning out and eating.

Cheesy Garlic Baguette

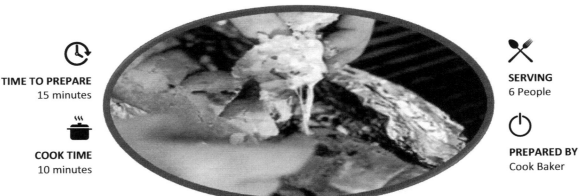

TIME TO PREPARE
15 minutes

COOK TIME
10 minutes

SERVING
6 People

PREPARED BY
Cook Baker

Ingredients

- ✓ 125g mozzarella ball
- ✓ 140g taleggio cheese , rind removed
- ✓ 100g butter , softened
- ✓ 3 garlic cloves , finely chopped
- ✓ handful parsley leaves, chopped
- ✓ 1 tsp fresh marjoram leaves, chopped, optional
- ✓ 1 long baguette
- ✓ large pinch of paprika

Steps to Cook

1. Light the barbecue. Chop the mozzarella and taleggio into small chunks and tip into a bowl with the butter, garlic, herbs and some salt and pepper. If you want, you can mix everything together with a wooden spoon, but I prefer to use my hands.

2. Using a bread knife, cut diagonal slices along the loaf about three quarters of the way into the bread – don't cut all the way through. If it looks like the bread won't fit on the barbecue, cut it in half and make two smaller ones.

3. Push the garlic butter generously between each cut, allowing some to ooze onto the top – it will caramelise and taste superb. Sprinkle the paprika over. Wrap the bread up like a cracker in a double thickness of foil. You can prepare to this stage up to a day ahead.

4. Put the pack straight onto the barbecue. Cook for 2 minutes then roll it over onto its side and cook for 2 minutes more. Roll it onto its other side and cook for a further 2 minutes. Have a peek – if the cheese is melting and the bread is crispy, remove it from the barbie. Pull the slices apart and eat while hot and gooey.

Cheese & Pesto Whirls

TIME TO PREPARE
40 minutes

COOK TIME
40 minutes

SERVING
12 People

PREPARED BY
Cook Baker

Ingredients

- ✓ 450g strong white bread flour, plus a little for dusting

- ✓ 7g sachet fast-action dried yeast

- ✓ 1 tsp golden caster sugar

- ✓ 2 tbsp olive oil, plus a drizzle

- ✓ 150g tub fresh pesto

- ✓ 240g tub semi-dried tomatoes, drained and roughly chopped

- ✓ 100g grated mozzarella (ready-grated is best for this, as it is drier than fresh)

- ✓ 50g parmesan (or vegetarian alternative), grated

- ✓ handful basil leaves

Steps to Cook

1   Merge the flour, yeast, sugar and 1 ½ tsp fine salt in a large mixing bowl, or the bowl of a tabletop mixer. Measure out 300ml warm water and add roughly 280ml to the flour, along with the olive oil, and start mixing until the ingredients start to clump together as a dough. If the dough seems a little dry, add the remaining water. Once Merged, knead for 10 mins by hand on your work surface, or for 5 mins on a medium speed in a mixer. The dough is ready when it feels soft, springy and elastic. Clean the bowl, drizzle in a little oil, then pop the dough back in, turning it over and coating the sides of the bowl in oil. Cover with some oiled cling film and set aside in a warm place to double in size – this will take 1-3 hrs, depending on the temperature.

2   Line a baking tray with parchment. Uncover the dough and punch it down a couple of times with your fist, knocking out all the air bubbles. Tip out onto a floured work surface and dust the top with a little flour too, if it is sticky. Roll the dough out to a rectangle, roughly 40 x 30cm. Spread the pesto over the dough, then scatter over the tomatoes, both cheeses and the basil. Roll the dough up from one of the longer sides, into a long sausage.

3   Use a sharp knife to cut the dough into 12 even pieces. Place on the baking tray, cut-side up, in a 3-by-4 formation, making sure the open end of each roll is tucked in towards the centre on the arrangement – this will prevent them from uncoiling during cooking. Leave a little space between each roll as they will grow and touch as they prove. Loosely cover with oiled cling film and leave to prove for 30 mins–1 hr until almost doubled in size again. Heat oven to 200C/180C fan/gas 6.

4   Uncover the bread when it is puffed up. Bake on the middle shelf in the oven for 35-40 mins until golden brown and the centre looks dry and not doughy. Remove from the oven and leave to cool for at least 10 mins.

Cheese Roll-ups

TIME TO PREPARE
30 minutes

COOK TIME
25 minutes

SERVING
6 People

PREPARED BY
Cook Baker

Ingredients

- ✓ 200g self-raising flour , plus extra for dusting
- ✓ 50g butter , softened
- ✓ 1 tsp paprika
- ✓ 100-125ml/3½-4fl oz milk
- ✓ 50g ready-grated mature cheddar

Steps to Cook

1 Heat oven to 220C/200C fan/gas 7. Put the flour and butter in a bowl and rub them together with your fingers. Rubbing in mixture with cold butter is hard and tiring on young fingers, so use slightly softened butter – but not so soft that it is oily. Now stir in the paprika and mix again.

2 Add 100ml milk and mix with a fork until you get a soft dough. Add a splash more milk if the dough is dry. This process will teach you how to feel the dough and decide if it needs more liquid. You can always add more milk if required.

3 On a lightly floured surface, roll out the dough like pastry to about 0.5cm thick. Try to keep a rectangular shape. Only roll in one direction, and roll and turn, roll and turn – by keeping the dough moving, you avoid finding it stuck at the end.

4 Sprinkle the grated cheese on top, then roll up like a sausage along the long side. Cut into 12 thick rings using a table knife. Get an adult to show you how to hold the dough with one hand and cut straight through with the other.

5 Line the baking tray with baking parchment. Place the roll-ups on the parchment, cut-side down, almost touching each other, making sure that you can see the spiral. Get an adult to put them in the oven for you and bake for 20-25 mins until golden and melty. Ask an adult to remove them from the oven, then leave to cool. The cheese roll-ups will keep for up to 3 days in an airtight container.

Tiger Bread

TIME TO PREPARE
25 minutes

COOK TIME
35 minutes

SERVING
6 People

PREPARED BY
Cook Baker

Ingredients

- ✓ 500g strong white bread flour, plus extra for kneading
- ✓ 7g sachet fast action yeast
- ✓ 1½ tsp caster sugar
- ✓ 1½ tsp fine sea salt
- ✓ 300-350ml warm water
- ✓ vegetable oil, for the bowl
- ✓ For the topping
- ✓ 90g rice flour
- ✓ ½ x 7g sachet fast action yeast
- ✓ ¼ tsp salt
- ✓ 1 tsp golden caster sugar
- ✓ ½ tbsp toasted sesame oil
- ✓ 90ml warm water

Steps to Cook

1 Tip the flour into a large mixing bowl. Stir through the yeast, sugar and salt. Make a well in the middle and gradually pour in the water. Swiftly mix together, then turn out onto a lightly floured surface. Knead the bread for 8-10 mins or until smooth and elastic. Lightly oil a large mixing bowl, then put the dough in the bowl, cover and leave in a warm place for 1 hr or until doubled in size.

2 Once the dough has risen, tip it onto a worktop and knead it three times. Shape the dough into an oval as best you can. Lightly flour a baking sheet and sit the loaf on it. Cover loosely with lightly oiled cling film and leave for a further 45 mins-1 hr or until doubled in size again.

3 Heat oven to 200C/180C fan/gas 6. Mix together all of the topping ingredients in a small bowl until you get a spreadable paste, adding more water and/or flour if necessary, then set aside to rest for 5 mins. Gently spread the mixture over the loaf with a palette knife. Place the baking sheet in the centre of the oven and bake for 35 mins. Once cooked, the loaf should sound hollow when the base is tapped and should feel light for its size. Leave to cool completely before cutting into slices.

Triangular Bread Thins

TIME TO PREPARE
8 minutes

COOK TIME
12 minutes

SERVING
6 People

PREPARED BY
Cook Baker

Ingredients

- ✓ 190g plain wholemeal spelt flour , plus extra for dusting
- ✓ ½ tsp bicarbonate of soda
- ✓ 1 tsp baking powder
- ✓ 75ml live bio yogurt made up to 150ml with cold water

Steps to Cook

1 Heat oven to 200C/180C fan/gas 6 and line a baking sheet with baking parchment. Mix the flour, bicarbonate of soda and baking powder in a bowl, then stir in the diluted yogurt with the blade of a knife until you have a soft, sticky dough, adding a little water if the mix is dry.

2 Tip the dough onto a lightly floured surface and shape and flatten with your hands to make a 20cm round. Take care not to over-handle as it can make the bread tough. Lift onto the baking sheet and cut into six triangles, slightly easing them apart with the knife. Bake for about 10-12 mins – they don't have to be golden, but should feel firm. Leave to cool on a wire rack.

3 Use to make our wild salmon & avocado triangles and goat's cheese, tomato & olive triangles. The rest can be packed into a food bag to use later in the week, or frozen until needed.

ù

Cheesy bonfire bread

TIME TO PREPARE
10 minutes

COOK TIME
30 minutes

SERVING
6 People

PREPARED BY
Cook Baker

Ingredients

- ✓ 200g wholemeal flour
- ✓ 200g plain flour , plus extra for dusting
- ✓ 1 tsp bicarbonate of soda
- ✓ 2 tsp cream of tartar
- ✓ 1 tsp salt
- ✓ 1 tsp caster sugar
- ✓ 25g butter , melted
- ✓ 300ml milk , at room temperature
- ✓ 175g cheddar , coarsely grated
- ✓ 3 tbsp pumpkin seeds
- ✓ 85g ready-roasted pepper from a jar, drained and chopped

Steps to Cook

1 Heat oven to 190C/170C fan/gas 5. Sift the dry ingredients into a large bowl and make a large well in the middle. Merge the melted butter and milk, then pour into the well. Mix to a soft dough.

2 Dust the work surface with flour. Add most of the cheddar, 2 tbsp of the pumpkin seeds and the chopped peppers to the dough. Gently knead to Merge on the floured surface. Divide into eight lumps and shape into rough rounds two finger-widths deep.

3 Put the pieces side by side on a floured baking sheet, scatter the remaining cheddar and pumpkin seeds over the top and bake for 30 mins until golden brown and the cheese is bubbling. Cool on a wire rack and eat while warm. Can be frozen at this point. To reheat, wrap the bread tightly in foil and bake at 200C/180C fan/gas 6 for about 30 mins.

Easy Bread Rolls

TIME TO PREPARE
30 minutes

COOK TIME
30 minutes

SERVING
8 People

PREPARED BY
Cook Baker

Ingredients

- ✓ 500g strong white bread flour , plus extra for dusting

- ✓ 7g sachet fast action yeast

- ✓ 1 tsp white caster sugar

- ✓ 2 tsp fine salt

- ✓ 1 tsp sunflower oil , plus extra for the work surface and bowl

Steps to Cook

1   Tip the flour, yeast, sugar, salt and oil into a bowl. Pour over 325ml warm water, then mix (with a spatula or your hand), until it comes together as a shaggy dough. Make sure all the flour has been incorporated. Cover and leave for 10 mins.

2   Lightly oil your work surface and tip the dough onto it. Knead the dough for at least 10 mins until it becomes tighter and springy – if you have a stand mixer you can do this with a dough hook for 5 mins. Pull the dough into a ball and put in a clean, oiled bowl. Leave for 1 hr, or until doubled in size.

3   Tip the dough onto a lightly floured surface and roll into a long sausage shape. Halve the dough, then divide each half into four pieces, so you have eight equal-sized portions. Roll each into a tight ball and put on a dusted baking tray, leaving some room between each ball for rising. Cover with a damp tea towel and leave in a warm place to prove for 40 mins-1 hr or until almost doubled in size.

4   Heat the oven to 230C/210C fan/gas 8. When the dough is ready, dust each ball with a bit more flour. (If you like, you can glaze the rolls with milk or beaten egg, and top with seeds.) Bake for 25-30mins, until light brown and hollow sounding when tapped on the base. Leave to cool on a wire rack.

Meatball & Garlic Bread Traybake

TIME TO PREPARE
10 minutes

COOK TIME
50 minutes

SERVING
3 People

PREPARED BY
Cook Baker

Ingredients

- ✓ 350g turkey thigh mince
- ✓ 1 tsp dried oregano
- ✓ 1 tsp fennel seeds
- ✓ 1½ tbsp olive oil
- ✓ 1 large onion , chopped
- ✓ 3 garlic cloves , crushed
- ✓ 1 tbsp tomato purée
- ✓ 2 x 400g cans chopped tomatoes
- ✓ 2 tsp sugar
- ✓ 150g ball mozzarella , torn into pieces
- ✓ 4 garlic breadsticks or garlic bread slices, torn or chopped into chunks
- ✓ 25g cheddar , grated
- ✓ green salad or spaghetti, to serve

Steps to Cook

1 Merge the mince, oregano, fennel seeds and some seasoning in a bowl. Take walnut-sized pieces of the mixture and roll into balls. Heat half the oil in a large, shallow ovenproof pan and cook the meatballs until browned all over – don't worry if they're not cooked through. Transfer to a plate. Heat the oven to 200C/180C fan/gas 6.

2 Heat the remaining oil in the pan and add the onion. Cook until softened, about 10-12 mins, stirring regularly. Stir in the garlic for another minute, then the tomato purée, chopped tomatoes and sugar.

3 Simmer for 10-15 mins, then season to taste. Place the meatballs on top of the sauce, then add the mozzarella, garlic bread and the cheddar on top. Bake for 15-20 mins until golden and crisp.

Naan Bread

TIME TO PREPARE
20 minutes

COOK TIME
35 minutes

SERVING
6 People

PREPARED BY
Cook Baker

Ingredients

- ✓ 1x 7g sachet dried yeast
- ✓ 2 tsp golden caster sugar
- ✓ 300g strong white bread flour, plus extra for dusting
- ✓ ½ tsp baking powder
- ✓ 25g butter or ghee, melted, plus extra 2-3 tbsp for the tray and brushing
- ✓ 150ml natural yogurt
- ✓ 1 tbsp nigella seeds

Steps to Cook

1   Put 125ml warm water into a bowl and sprinkle over the yeast and 1 tsp of the sugar. Leave for 10-15 mins or until frothy. In a larger bowl, put the flour, remaining sugar, ½ tsp salt and baking powder. Mix together then make a well in the centre in which to pour the melted butter, yogurt, nigella seeds and yeast mixture. Stir well, then start to bring the mixture together with your hands. If it's very wet add a spoonful of flour but if it's dry add a splash more warm water. It should be a very soft dough but not so wet that it won't come together into a ball.

2   When you're happy with the consistency, start kneading, first in the bowl, then transfer the mixture onto a well-floured surface and continue to knead for 10 mins or until smooth and elastic but still soft. Butter a large bowl, then shape the dough into a ball and place in the prepared bowl. Cover and leave in a warm place for about 1 hr or until doubled in size.

3   Divide the dough into six balls and put them on a baking tray dusted with flour, then cover the tray with a damp tea towel. Heat a large non-stick frying pan over a high heat. Take one of the balls of dough and roll it out to form a teardrop shape that's approximately 21cm long and around 13cm at the widest part. When the pan is very hot, carefully lay the naan bread into it. Let it dry fry and puff up for about 3 mins, then turn over and cook on the other side for another 3-4 mins or until cooked through and charred in patches.

4   Heat the oven to its lowest setting and put the cooked naan bread on a baking sheet. Brush with a little melted butter and cover with foil. Keep warm in the oven and layer up the cooked naans one on top of each other as you make them, brushing each one with melted butter or ghee as you go. Serve warm with curry or dips.

Vegan Banana Bread

TIME TO PREPARE
10 minutes

COOK TIME
40 minutes

SERVING
8 People

PREPARED BY
Cook Baker

Ingredients

- ✓ 3 large black bananas
- ✓ 75ml vegetable oil or sunflower oil, plus extra for the tin
- ✓ 100g brown sugar
- ✓ 225g plain flour (or use self-raising flour and reduce the baking powder to 2 heaped tsp)
- ✓ 3 heaped tsp baking powder
- ✓ 3 tsp cinnamon or mixed spice
- ✓ 50g dried fruit or nuts (optional)

Steps to Cook

1 Heat oven to 200C/180C fan/gas 6. Mash 3 large black peeled bananas with a fork, then mix well with 75g vegetable or sunflower oil and 100g brown sugar.

2 Add 225g plain flour, 3 heaped tsp baking powder and 3 tsp cinnamon or mixed spice, and Merge well. Add 50g dried fruit or nuts, if using.

3 Bake in an oiled, lined 2lb loaf tin for 20 minutes. Check and cover with foil if the cake is browning.

4 Bake for another 20 minutes, or until a skewer comes out clean.

5 Allow to cool a little before slicing. It's delicious freshly baked, but develops a lovely gooey quality the day after.

Peach Bread

TIME TO PREPARE
20 minutes

COOK TIME
45 minutes

SERVING
6 People

PREPARED BY
Cook Baker

Ingredients

- ✓ 3 cups fresh peaches
- ✓ 4 ounces butter (soft)
- ✓ 3 large eggs
- ✓ 2 tsp vanilla
- ✓ 1 cup sugar (granulated)
- ✓ 2 cups flour (white)
- ✓ 2 tsp. cinnamon
- ✓ 1 1/2 tsp. baking powder
- ✓ 1/2 tsp. baking soda
- ✓ 1/4 tsp. salt
- ✓ turbinado sugar for garnish (optional)

Steps to Cook

Preheat oven to 350 degrees F

Take butter out to soften

Wash, peel and chop 3 cups of peaches (set to side until needed)

Wash peel and slice a few peaches for the top (set to side until needed)

Merge all wet ingredients in a large bowl

Add softened butter to 1 cup of sugar in a mixing bowl and stir

Add in eggs, 2 tsp. vanilla and stir together.

In a separate bowl add dry ingredients

Measure and add flour, baking powder, baking soda, salt and cinnamon to bowl

Slowly Mix together

Then add the flour mixture to the wet ingredients while mixing (Don't over mix)

When fully Merged add peaches and stir in.

Add ingredients into your prepared baking dish

Pre-spray your bread pan with Pam and add about a tbsp. of flour move around covering all sides of your pan (add more only if needed)

Shake out excess flour

Pour your mixture into your prepared pan

Add your sliced, peeled peaches into the top of the batter across the loaf. Slightly pressing the slices in.

Sprinkle with cinnamon and turbinado sugar.

16   Bake until done (50-60 minutes

Pumpkin Bread

TIME TO PREPARE
15 minutes

COOK TIME
60 minutes

SERVING
4 People

PREPARED BY
Cook Baker

Ingredients

- ✓ 2 eggs
- ✓ 1/2 cup butter
- ✓ 1 cup fresh or canned pumpkin puree
- ✓ 1 cup light brown sugar
- ✓ 2 tsp. cinnamon
- ✓ 1 tsp. pumpkin spice
- ✓ 1/2 tsp. salt
- ✓ 1 tsp. baking powder
- ✓ 1 tsp. baking soda
- ✓ 1-1/2 cups white flour
- ✓ non-stick spray for preparing pan (Pam)
- ✓ 2 tbsp. flour for preparing pan

Steps to Cook

1 Mix softened butter, 2 eggs, pumpkin puree and light brown sugar in your mixing bowl or mixer.

2 In a separate bowl - add all your dry ingredients together and gently mix all ingredients by hand to distribute dry ingredients.

3 Slowly add mixed dry ingredients to your mixer or bowl with already creamed wet ingredients. DO NOT OVER MIX!

4 Preheat oven to 350 degrees.

5 Prepare your baking pan by spraying with a non stick spray. Add a little flour and move around your baking pan to cover sides. Shake out excess flour.

6 Add your mixed batter to your baking loaf pan.

7 Set your pan in the oven to bake it. It will take 45-60 minutes. Use a knife or tooth pick to see when it comes out clean. But, don't over bake. You will have to keep checking during the last 20 minutes.

8 Let cool slightly before removing from pan. You can use a knife along the sides if needed to loosen edges of baked pumpkin bread then... (be careful if you use a non stick pan this could scratch the sides. Try to remove bread from pan it first before doing this.)

9 Take a plate and place it over your baking dish and flip it over.

10 Serve with coffee and add butter to the top if desired.

Zucchini Bread

TIME TO PREPARE
15 minutes

COOK TIME
50 minutes

SERVING
6 People

PREPARED BY
Cook Baker

Ingredients

- ✓ 1 1/2- 2 cup shredded raw zucchini 2-4 zucchini
- ✓ 1/2 cup peeled shredded or chopped apple
- ✓ 1 1/2 cups all-purpose flour
- ✓ 1 teaspoon baking soda
- ✓ 1/4 teaspoon baking powder
- ✓ 1/4 teaspoon salt
- ✓ 1 teaspoon ground cinnamon
- ✓ 1/2 cup vegetable oil
- ✓ 1/2 cup granulated white sugar
- ✓ 1/2 cup light brown sugar
- ✓ 2 large eggs
- ✓ 1 teaspoon pure vanilla extract
- ✓ 1/2 cup chopped pecans are optional

Steps to Cook

1 How to make zucchini bread

2 Add flour, baking powder, baking soda, cinnamon, salt into a medium-size bowl. Stir together gently then set to the side.

3 Add oil, eggs, vanilla, sugar together in a large bowl and stir together.

4 Slowly add in dry ingredients into your mixed wet ingredients. When all the flour mixture is mixed in go to the next step.

5 Gently stir in the shredded zucchini. And optional chopped pecans.

6 Add your mixture into a prepared loaf pan when incorporated.

7 Bake at 350 degrees about 50 minutes or until done.

8 Check on the baking zucchini bread 15 minutes prior to the end time. This way will help you determine how much longer it will need to cook. Adjust the baking time as needed.

9 When done remove from oven and let cool slightly.

10 Invert pan, slice, and enjoy!

Pan de Muertos

TIME TO PREPARE
10 minutes

COOK TIME
60 minutes

SERVING
4 People

PREPARED BY
Cook Baker

Ingredients

- ✓ 1/4 cup butter
- ✓ 1/4 cup milk
- ✓ 1/4 cup warm water
- ✓ 3 cups all purpose flour
- ✓ 1 1/4 tsp active dry yeast
- ✓ 1/2 tsp salt
- ✓ 2 tsp anise seed
- ✓ 1/4 cup white sugar
- ✓ 2 eggs beaten
- ✓ 2 tsp orange zest
- ✓ 1/4 cup white sugar
- ✓ 1/4 cup orange juice
- ✓ 1 tbsp orange zest
- ✓ 2 tbsp white sugar

Steps to Cook

1   In a small saucepan, heat milk and butter over medium heat.

2   Remove from heat once the butter has melted, add the warm water...the mixture should be about 110F.

3   In a large bowl Merge 1/2 cup flour, yeast, salt, anise seed, 1/4 cup sugar.

4   Add wet ingredients to dry.

5   Once Merged, add beaten eggs and orange zest

6   Add 1/2 cup of flour and continue adding flour until dough has formed and is soft.

7   Place dough on lightly floured surface and knead until smooth.

8   Lightly grease a large bowl with olive oil, place the ball of dough inside greased bowl...cover with plastic wrap and place in a warm, dry spot until dough has doubled in size...about 1 hour.

9   After 1 hour, punch down ball of dough and place ball on a parchment lined baking sheet.

10 Cut away a few pieces that can be shaped into bones and place on top of ball of dough.

11 Once decorated, cover with plastic wrap and allow to rise again for another hour.

12 After the second rise, remove the plastic wrap and place in a 350F oven for about 35-45 minutes...until golden brown.

13 To make glaze; Merge orange juice, 1/4 sugar and zest in a small sauce pan...bring to boil...brush over top of the still warm bread...sprinkle with 2 tbsp sugar.

Buttermilk Bread Recipe with Honey

TIME TO PREPARE
200 minutes

COOK TIME
20 minutes

SERVING
6 People

PREPARED BY
Cook Baker

Ingredients

✓ 1 cup (240ml) whole milk, warmed to about 110°F

✓ 2 and 1/4 teaspoons Red Star Platinum yeast (1 standard packet)

✓ 2 Tablespoons granulated sugar, divided

✓ 1 large egg

✓ 1/4 cup (60g) unsalted butter, softened to room temperature and cut into 4 pieces

✓ 1 teaspoon salt

✓ 3 cups (375g) all-purpose flour or bread flour (spoon & leveled)*

✓ optional topping: 2 Tablespoons melted unsalted butter mixed with 1 Tablespoon honey

Steps to Cook

1   Prepare the dough: Mix the warm milk, yeast, and 1 Tablespoon of sugar together in the bowl of your stand mixer fitted with a dough hook or paddle attachment. Cover and allow to sit for 5 minutes.

2   Add the remaining sugar, egg, butter, salt, and 1 cup flour. Beat on low speed for 30 seconds, scrape down the sides of the bowl with a rubber spatula, then add the remaining flour. Beat on medium speed until the dough comes together and pulls away from the sides of the bowl, about 2 minutes. *If you do not own a mixer, you can mix this dough with a large wooden spoon or rubber spatula. It will take a bit of arm muscle!*

3   Knead the dough: Keep the dough in the mixer and beat for an additional 2 minutes or knead by hand on a lightly floured surface for 2 minutes. (See video tutorial above if you need a visual of kneading dough by hand.)

4   1st Rise: Lightly grease a large bowl with oil or nonstick spray. Place the dough in the bowl, turning it to coat all sides in the oil. Cover the bowl with aluminum foil, plastic wrap, or a clean kitchen towel. Allow the dough to rise in a relatively warm environment for 1-2 hours or until double in size. (I always let it rise on the counter. Takes about 2 hours. For a tiny reduction in rise time, see my answer to Where Should Dough Rise? in my Baking with Yeast Guide.)

5   Grease a 9×13 inch baking pan or two 9-inch square or round baking pans. You can also bake the rolls in a cast iron skillet or on a lined baking sheet.*

6   Shape the rolls: When the dough is ready, punch it down to release the air. Divide the dough into 14-16 equal pieces. (Just eyeball it– doesn't need to be perfect!) Shape each piece into a smooth ball. I do this entirely in my hands and you can watch in the video tutorial above. Arrange in prepared baking pan.

7   2nd Rise: Cover shaped rolls with aluminum foil, plastic wrap, or a clean kitchen towel. Allow to rise until puffy, about 1 hour.

8   Adjust oven rack to a lower position and preheat oven to 350°F (177°C). (It's best to bake the rolls towards the bottom of the oven so the tops don't burn.)

9   Bake the rolls: Bake for 20-25 minutes or until golden brown on top, rotating the pan halfway through. If you notice the tops browning too quickly, loosely tent the pan with aluminum foil. Remove from the oven, brush with optional honey butter topping, and allow rolls to cool for a few minutes before serving.

10   Cover leftover rolls tightly and store at room temperature for 2-3 days or in the refrigerator for up to 1 week.

Easy Soda Bread

TIME TO PREPARE
5 minutes

COOK TIME
40 minutes

SERVING
4 People

PREPARED BY
Cook Baker

Ingredients

- ✓ 500g plain wholemeal flour
- ✓ 2 tsp sea salt
- ✓ 1 tsp bicarbonate of soda
- ✓ 1 tbsp finely chopped rosemary (optional)
- ✓ 400ml whole milk
- ✓ 1 lemon, juiced
- ✓ 2 tsp honey

Steps to Cook

1 Heat oven to 200C/180C fan/gas 6. Mix together the flour, salt and bicarb in a bowl. And if you'd like rosemary bread, add the chopped rosemary too.

2 Mix together the milk and lemon juice in a jug, and wait for a minute as it magically turns into buttermilk. Then stir in the honey, and simply pour it into the flour mixture. Stir it with a knife for a minute until the whole thing comes together into a sticky dough.

3 Tip onto a floured work surface and shape it into a ball.

4 Put the ball on a floured baking tray and, using a sharp knife, make a deep cross on top.

5 Put in the oven and bake for 40 mins.

6 Cool on a wire rack until warm, then slice and serve.

Focaccia

TIME TO PREPARE
20 minutes

COOK TIME
25 minutes

SERVING
4 People

PREPARED BY
Cook Baker

Ingredients

- ✓ 500g strong bread flour , plus extra for dusting
- ✓ 7g dried fast action yeast
- ✓ 2 tsp fine sea salt
- ✓ 5 tbsp olive oil , plus extra for the tin and to serve
- ✓ 1 tsp flaky sea salt
- ✓ ¼ small bunch of rosemary , sprigs picked

Steps to Cook

1 Tip the flour into a large mixing bowl. Mix the yeast into one side of the flour, and the fine salt into the other side. Then mix everything together, this initial seperation prevents the salt from killing the yeast.

2 Make a well in the middle of the flour and add 2 tbsp oil and 350-400ml lukewarm water, adding it gradually until you have a slightly sticky dough (you may not need all the water). Sprinkle the work surface with flour and tip the dough onto it, scraping around the sides of the bowl. Knead for 5-10 mins until your dough is soft and less sticky. Put the dough into a clean bowl, cover with a tea towel and leave to prove for 1 hr until doubled in size.

3 Oil a rectangle, shallow tin (25 x 35cm). Tip the dough onto the work surface, then stretch it to fill the tin. Cover with a tea towel and leave to prove for another 35-45 mins.

4 Heat the oven to 220C/200C fan/gas 7. Press your fingers into the dough to make dimples. Mix together 1½ tbsp olive oil, 1 tbsp water and the flaky salt and drizzle over the bread. Push sprigs of rosemary into the dimples in the dough.

5 Bake for 20 mins until golden. Whilst the bread is still hot, drizzle over 1-2 tbsp olive oil. Cut into squares and serve warm or cold with extra olive oil, if you like.

Potato & Turmeric Focaccia

TIME TO PREPARE
20 minutes

COOK TIME
30 minutes

SERVING
6 People

PREPARED BY
Cook Baker

Ingredients

- ✓ 1 tsp fresh yeast , or ½ tsp fast-action dried yeast
- ✓ 2 tbsp olive oil
- ✓ 450g organic strong white flour
- ✓ For the topping
- ✓ 3 medium waxy potatoes , thinly sliced
- ✓ 2 tbsp olive oil , plus extra to serve
- ✓ 1 tsp turmeric
- ✓ 1 rosemary sprig, leaves picked and chopped, to serve

Steps to Cook

1 In a large bowl, dissolve the yeast in 350ml cold water and add the oil. Add the flour and 1 tsp salt and mix thoroughly with your hands to make a dough. Cover and leave in the fridge or a cool place overnight.

2 The next day, turn your dough out onto an oiled tray approx 30cm x 20cm. Using your fingertips, gently stretch the dough into a rectangle, then fold it in half. Rotate the dough 90 degrees and repeat the process. Leave to rest for 30 mins. Repeat this stretching, folding and resting process twice more.

3 Heat oven to 24OC/220C fan/gas 9. Gently stretch the dough to fill your tray. If it shrinks back, don't force it – rest for 10 more mins, then try again.

4 Spread the potato slices over the dough, overlapping. Mix the olive oil with the turmeric and brush over, then sprinkle with sea salt and bake on the top shelf of the oven for 25-30 mins. When cooked, drizzle with a little more olive oil and scatter over the rosemary.

Focaccia with Pesto & Mozzarella

TIME TO PREPARE
20 minutes

COOK TIME
30 minutes

SERVING
4 People

PREPARED BY
Cook Baker

Ingredients

- ✓ 500g strong white bread flour, plus some for dusting
- ✓ 1 ½ tsp salt
- ✓ 7g sachet fast-action yeast
- ✓ 2 tbsp extra-virgin olive oil , plus some for drizzling
- ✓ 125g ball mozzarella , drained
- ✓ 5 tbsp pesto (shop-bought or see recipe, below)
- ✓ sea salt , to serve (optional)

Steps to Cook

1. Put the flour into a bowl and mix in the salt. Mix the yeast into 325ml tepid water. Add the water and oil to the flour, then mix well with a plastic scraper or your hands. When most of the liquid is incorporated, use your hands to bring all the ingredients together into a ball of dough.

2. Tip the dough out onto a worktop lightly dusted with flour and work it by pulling and stretching for at least 10 mins. Try to get as much air into it as possible. Put the ball of worked dough into a well-oiled bowl, cover with a little more oil and a tea towel or cling film. Leave to rest for 1 hr or so in a non-draughty warm spot, until doubled in size.

3. Now stretch the dough out onto a baking sheet until it's about 20 x 30cm. Leave the dough to rise again to about half as high again, about 30-40 mins in a warm draught-free place, loosely covered with a tea towel.

4. Heat oven to 180C/160C fan/gas 4. When the dough has risen, press your fingers into it gently to make some holes. Bake for about 15 mins, then remove from the oven. Tear over the mozzarella, then bake for another 5-10 mins until golden and cooked through. Drizzle over the pesto and scatter with sea salt, if you like. Serve straight away.

Artichoke Focaccia

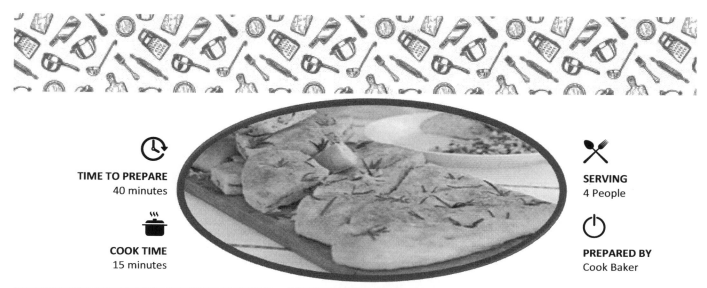

TIME TO PREPARE
40 minutes

COOK TIME
15 minutes

SERVING
4 People

PREPARED BY
Cook Baker

Ingredients

- ✓ 500g strong flour
- ✓ 7g sachet fast-action yeast
- ✓ 1 heaped tsp salt
- ✓ For the filling
- ✓ large bunch rosemary
- ✓ 285g jar artichoke antipasti in oil (we used Sacla)
- ✓ 50g freshly grated parmesan (or vegetarian alternative), plus extra for grating

Steps to Cook

1. Tip the flour into a large bowl and make a well in the centre. Add the yeast and salt, then gradually pour in 350ml tepid water, stirring as you go. Bring the dough together with a spoon, then with your hands. It should be soft, but not too sticky or wet. If it won't come together, pour in a little extra water; if the dough is too wet, add extra flour. Tip onto a floured work surface and knead for about 10 mins, or until it's smooth, soft and springs back when pushed with a finger. Leave to rise in an oiled bowl covered with cling film in a warm place for 1 hr or Packed with summer flavours until the dough has doubled in size.

2. Strip leaves from half the rosemary and finely chop. Break the rest into smaller pieces. Drain the artichokes, reserving the oil, and chop into chunks.

3. When risen, tip the dough onto an oiled work surface and roll out into a 35 x 45cm rectangle. Slip an oiled baking sheet under half of the dough. Top the half with artichokes, all the Parmesan and rosemary. Grind over black pepper and drizzle with a little of the reserved oil. Fold over the other dough half, pressing the edges together and under to seal. Leave to rise in a warm place, covered with the oiled cling film, for 30 mins. Heat oven to 240C/fan 220C/gas 9.

4. Drizzle with a little more of the oil and make dents in the top with your fingers. Pop the rosemary sprigs into the dents and grate over a little more cheese. Bake for 15 mins, until golden and risen. Cool on a rack for 30 mins, cut into squares and serve.

Pesto Focaccia Sandwich

TIME TO PREPARE
40 minutes

COOK TIME
30 minutes

SERVING
6 People

PREPARED BY
Cook Baker

Ingredients

- ✓ 500g strong white flour
- ✓ 7g fast-action yeast
- ✓ 2 tbsp olive oil , plus a little extra
- ✓ small pack basil , leaves picked
- ✓ 2 x 125g mozzarella balls
- ✓ 2 tbsp pine nuts , toasted
- ✓ 3 tbsp green pesto

Steps to Cook

1   Put the flour, yeast and 1 tsp salt in a large bowl, ensuring the yeast and salt don't touch. Pour in 350ml lukewarm water and the olive oil, and bring together with a spoon to form a wet, elastic dough. If using a stand mixer, knead for 5 mins or until the dough stops sticking to the side of the bowl. If kneading by hand, knead for 10 mins on a lightly floured surface.

2   Put the dough in a lightly oiled bowl, cover with a clean, damp tea towel and leave to rise for 1 hr or until doubled in size.

3   Line a 20 x 30cm roasting tin with a piece of crumpled baking parchment. Cut the dough in half and press, as lightly as possible, one half into the roasting tin, stretching it out to fill the tin. Cover with the basil, mozzarella and pine nuts, then spread out the other half of the dough and place on top. Cover and leave to rise for 1 hr or until light and puffy.

4   Meanwhile, heat oven to 200C/ 180C fan/gas 6. Once risen, press indents with your fingers into the top of the dough. The dough is ready if the indents stay; if they bounce back, leave the dough for longer. Fill the indents with pesto, then sprinkle with a little flaky sea salt and drizzle with a little olive oil.

5   Bake on the top shelf of the oven for 25-30 mins, without opening the oven door, until golden.

6   Transfer to a wire rack and leave to cool completely. Take to your picnic whole and slice into 10-12 sandwiches when serving.

Pitta bread

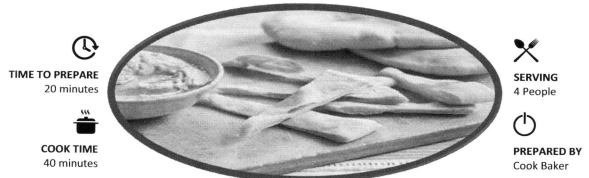

TIME TO PREPARE
20 minutes

COOK TIME
40 minutes

SERVING
4 People

PREPARED BY
Cook Baker

Ingredients

- ✓ 2 tsp fast-action dried yeast
- ✓ 500g strong white bread flour, plus extra for dusting
- ✓ 2 tsp salt
- ✓ 1 tbsp olive oil

Steps to Cook

1. Mix the yeast with 300ml warm water in a large bowl. Leave to sit for 5 mins until the yeast is super bubbly then tip in the flour, salt and olive oil. Bring the mixture together into a soft dough. Don't worry if it looks a little rough round the edges.

2. Tip the dough onto a lightly floured work surface. Knead for 5-10 mins until you have a soft, smooth and elastic dough. Try to knead using as little extra flour as possible, just enough so that the dough doesn't stick – this will keep the pittas light and airy. Once kneaded, place in a lightly oiled bowl, cover with a tea towel and leave to double in size, approximately 1 hour.

3. Heat oven as high as it will go (ideally 250C/230C fan/gas 9) and put a large baking tray on the middle shelf of the oven to get searingly hot. Divide the dough into eight balls then flatten each into a disc with the palm of your hand. On a lightly floured surface, roll each disc into an oval, around 20cm long, 15cm wide and 3-5mm thick

4. Carefully remove the hot tray from the oven. Dust with flour then place your pittas directly onto it – you may have to do this in batches. Return swiftly to the oven and bake for 4-5 mins, or until the pittas have puffed up and are a pale golden colour. Wrap each hot pitta in a clean tea towel once it's baked to keep it soft while the others cook.

Caramelised Onion Focaccia

TIME TO PREPARE
20 minutes

COOK TIME
60 minutes

SERVING
4 People

PREPARED BY
Cook Baker

Ingredients

- ✓ 250g '00' flour
- ✓ 250g strong white bread flour
- ✓ 7g sachet fast-action dried yeast
- ✓ 10g fine sea salt
- ✓ 3 tbsp good-quality olive oil , plus extra for drizzling
- ✓ knob of butter
- ✓ 3 large red onions , sliced
- ✓ 2 tbsp balsamic vinegar

Steps to Cook

1 Mix the flours with the yeast and salt, add 1 tbsp oil, then pour in 320ml lukewarm water and mix well. You want a very soft dough – don't worry if it looks a little wet, this will make a lighter focaccia. Knead for 5 mins if using a stand mixer, or 10 mins by hand, using a dough scraper if you have one and lightly oiling your hands and the surface. Transfer the dough to a lightly oiled bowl, cover with a damp tea towel and leave to rise until it has doubled in size.

2 Meanwhile, melt the butter in a large frying pan with the remaining oil, add the onions and a pinch of salt, and cook gently for 20 mins or until very soft. Pour in the vinegar and cook for a further 10 mins until sticky. Set aside to cool.

3 Oil an A4-sized roasting tin, scrape in the dough and reshape in the tin (see tip, below), gently pushing the dough into the corners. Scatter over the onions, cover with a piece of lightly oiled cling film and leave until puffed up.

4 Meanwhile, heat oven to 220C/200C fan/gas 7. Using your fingers, lightly dimple the dough all over, drizzle with a little oil and sprinkle with sea salt. Bake for 30 mins until golden brown. Can be made the day before and stored in an airtight container.

106

Red Onion & Rosemary Focaccia

TIME TO PREPARE
25 minutes

COOK TIME
40 minutes

SERVING
4 People

PREPARED BY
Cook Baker

Ingredients

- ✓ 1 batch white bread dough (see 'Goes well with' recipe below)
- ✓ 5 tbsp olive oil
- ✓ 2 large red onions, sliced
- ✓ handful rosemary sprigs
- ✓ 1 tsp sea salt flakes

Steps to Cook

1. Make the basic dough, adding 2 tbsp olive oil and only a pinch of salt. While the dough is rising, cook onions in 1 tbsp olive oil for 5 mins until soft, then set aside.

2. When the dough has risen, knock it back and stretch it to fit an oiled Swiss roll tin about 25 x 35cm. Leave the dough to prove for about 20 mins.

3. Heat oven to 200C/fan 180C/gas 6. Spread the onions over the dough and scatter with the rosemary. Press your fingers into the dough to make dimples, drizzle the remaining oil over and scatter over the salt, then bake for 30 mins until golden. Leave to cool, then serve cut or torn into squares.

Printed in Great Britain
by Amazon

87164818R00068